UNRELIABLE MEMORIES

Rummaging through my life

Blair Kesseler

Copyright © 2024 Blair Kesseler

All rights reserved

No part of this book may be reproduced, or stored in a retrieval system, or transmitted in any form or by any means, electronic, mechanical, photocopying, recording, or otherwise, without express written permission of the publisher.

ISBN 9798335532648

Cover design by: Blair Kesseler

PREFACE

There are a range of photographs that accompany each chapter of this book and they can be found at; unreliablememories.notion.site

CHAPTER 1 – GRANDMA AND GRANDAD

As I begin to write this, I am 77 years old. My family keep telling me that I should write down my memories before I forget them all! The problem is that I am not sure how accurate my memories are. However, I am going to try and record some of the events of my life, as I remember them.

I am entitling this memoir "Unreliable Memories". All the stories that I record here are true, at least I believe them to be true, which isn't the same thing at all! For example, my grandmother, Winifred Kesseler, was believed by the family to have been born in Portobello, on the coast just outside Edinburgh. I'm quite sure that she told me this herself, however, that would have been quite a feat since the census reveals that her parents were in Birmingham by this time! Unreliable memories. So, with that in mind, believe what you will from the stories that follow.

My parents were Edward Howard Kesseler and Mary Deffley. For the sake of chronology, we will begin with the stories of their parents, my grandparents.

My parental grandfather was Joseph Louis Kesseler, born in 1870 in Birmingham. His father was a merchant originally born in Germany whose name was Edward [anglicised from Edouard]. Joseph, or Joe as he was normally known, was one of 12 children, all born over the course of 20 years. Edouard had two wives, consecutively of course!

The family was Roman Catholic, but young Joe met and fell in love with a pretty waitress named Winifred McDonald. Winifred was five years younger than Joe being just 25 when they married at Saint James's church, Ashted, on Boxing Day 1900. Unfortunately for the family's future, Winifred was a Protestant and because of their marriage Joe was estranged from his family

Two years after the wedding, their first child, George was born to

1

be followed by Sydney in 1905, Edward in 1907 and finally Ruth in 1916.

FAMILY STORY ALERT. (This indicates a family story which may, or may not, be apocryphal. I have no reason to disbelieve it – but I cannot confirm it.) My dad was originally going to be named Howard McDonald Kesseler, to honour his Scottish ancestry. However, not long after his birth came a visitor from the East. The East of Birmingham, that is, and it wasn't a King, but his German born, semi-estranged grandfather. He arrived at the Coventry Street back-to-back house they lived in in a horse drawn carriage, entered the house and walked across to the baby. He gently placed a golden guinea in the child's hand and, turning to Winifred, said, "You will name him, Edward". With a 1907 Guinea being worth around £395 now, I think she would have named him after one of the horses, if asked! But Edward Howard it became, and the name Edward MacDonald wasn't used until my brother was born.

This story indicates that the gulf between the Catholic and Protestant families had eased by 1907. I understand that Eduoard (always known as 'The German' in the family) became quite fond of his daughter-in-law who he called 'Vinifer'.

My grandfather, Joe, was a baker and, by reputation, a good one. In 1910 he was prevailed on by his fellow employees to lead a strike against his employers for better wages. The claim, I believe was for an extra farthing a week. (Note to younger readers, look it up on Google – a farthing was the smallest coin of the realm). The strike was settled, and the employers agreed to pay the workers their claim on one condition, that Joseph Kesseler was sacked! Solidarity disappeared at the prospect of extra money and Joe found himself without a job. Not only unemployed but black-listed, no baker in the Midlands would employ him. **FAMILY STORY ALERT**. Apparently, he eventually found a job in Llandudno, even though even there they knew about him being a 'troublemaker.

In 1914, the first war against Germany began and Joe joined up. He didn't have to, he was 44 years old, but he lied about his age in order to enlist. He also gave his name as Louis Joseph Kesseler, but I can't believe that this attempt at subterfuge would be successful. I think the truth was the Army was happy to take anyone who offered.

FAMILY STORY ALERT. Joe's war record was a mystery until recently. Most of us believed that he never left England and that he looked after horses. There is a portrait photograph of him sitting astride a horse in my office at home. I always believed the story that this was an officer's horse he looked after and rented out for photographs to send home. It does somehow ring true as something he would have done.

However, I recently obtained his war record and found out that, not only did he serve in France, but he was eventually discharged on medical grounds and awarded a small pension. The medical grounds are not obvious but are likely to be shell shock related. He, like many of his generation, never mentioned his service.

On returning to civilian life, he again got employment as a baker, a profession he would follow for the rest of his life. Indeed, he continued working until 1954. By this time, he was working for a local bakery that was taken over by a national conglomerate. Not long after the take-over Joe was stopped by a new, young manager on a staircase. The manager asked who he was, "Joe Kesseler, sir", he replied. "Mr. Kesseler, can I ask how old you are? ", asked the manager. Joe guessed he might be in trouble, so he lied. "I'm 74, sir.", he said. The manager looked concerned and explained that their insurance didn't cover anyone over 70 and they would have to let him go, with immediate effect. "On that basis,", said Joe, "I'm really 84!", and he left.

By this time, I was 10 and would often have Sunday lunch with my grandparents. It was obvious that Joe missed the camaraderie of the workplace but made up for it by regular visits to the 'Lea Hall Tavern' or 'The Ring O' Bells', his favourite pub in Church Road, Yardley. He wasn't a big drinker, but he did like the company. This involved a bus journey on the number 16 from Whittington Oval. When returning and worried about his failing eyesight, he would often walk from the bus to home (400 yards or so) in the centre of the road so that he wouldn't trip over the curb.

He died, age 90, in 1960, following a morning visit to the pub. Coming home feeling a little tired, he decided to have an afternoon kip in his bed. There was a heater at the side of the bed, which was making the room uncomfortable hot, so he leaned over to switch it off, fell and hit his head. For the next few days, he slipped in and out of consciousness, always with one of his children by his side, until he finally passed away. The Catholic side of the family were concerned for his soul and sent a priest round to the house. He was politely turned away.

My recollections of him always make me smile. He was a jolly man, with a sense of mischievousness. He would say things to me that Grandma would think inappropriate, and she would admonish him with, "Joe, what will the boy think of us?". He had a special twinkle in the eye, and I thought the world of him.

Winnie, my grandmother was just a lovely but much more reserved than granddad. She was a good Christian lady, and I use all three adjectives wisely. She was, by denomination, an Anglican but often worshipped at a Medical Mission in Lea Hall, close to where she lived. Her faith was a great influence on mine and that tin hut church was the first free church that I ever worshipped in. We will come to my ongoing faith journey later in the journal.

Photographs show what a strikingly beautiful woman Winifred was when young, but even when I knew her as an older lady, she was impressive. Well turned out and always clean and tidy, unless she was gardening. Gardening was her passion, mainly fruit and vegetables. Great towers of sprouts grew in the front garden and the borders were filled with bunches of chives, flowering purple in season. Cabbages and onions in the back. The only flowers I remember were 'red hot pokers' (Kniphofia) although there may have been more.

FAMILY STORY ALERT. Grandma was different to everyone else I knew in that she only had one hand. The story was that she lost the other because of her gardening. One day she turned up a rusty nail and it pierced her hand. Later it 'went bad ways' and the hand had to be amputated. She was fitted with an artificial hand that was attached to a leather cup that went over the stump. The hand, which wore a grey glove and was shaped so that it could carry a handbag, clicked onto this cup. The problem was that when attached, it was a good three inches longer than the other arm. This made Grandma very self-conscious, and she would always try to hide it behind her back if photographed.

Of course, to a 10-year-old, this was nothing special, it was just the way Grandma was. One day, she and I were boarding a number 14 bus when, halfway up the aisle, her hand fell off. It started to roll back towards the platform, which in those days had no doors. I happily chased after, shouting, "It's OK Granny, I'll get it for you'. She, embarrassed beyond measure, ignored it, and sat down. My abiding memory of the event was the look on the faces of the other passengers and the conductor.

She would never have classed herself as disabled. She could do almost everything she needed to do. I remember her peeling potatoes and I challenge anybody else to try that using only one hand. It was at her house in Loeless Road where I first started to cook, encouraged by her. She loved my fluffy omelette.

She never really recovered from losing her husband and died 18 months after him in 1962.

I feel very fortunate to have known these special people who had a great influence on me. They passed on many of their special qualities to their four children and I will come back to my uncles and aunt later. I have no doubt that Winnie and Joe will also crop up again.

CHAPTER 2 – NAN

My maternal grandmother was Jane Deffley who was born as Jane Cooper in 1887. She was the daughter of John Cooper and his wife Elizabeth Cole.

Jane, usually known as Jinnie, was the oldest of three daughters the others being Mary and Elizabeth. Mary, for some reason was known as Polly and Elizabeth always as Liz. Like so many of my ancestors, they lived in the Digbeth/Deritend area of Birmingham.

Jinnie married William Deffley on the first of August 1909 in their local Anglican Church in Heath Mill Lane, Deritend. The church was St. Basils, a place that turns up much later in my life. My mother, Mary, was born later that year and her sister, Lily in 1915. Four years after Lily's birth Jane's husband died, leaving her with two small children and a widowed father to care for.

I always knew her as Nan and, except for my wife, she was the most important woman in my life. The most caring, loving, and generous person I have ever met.

Her life was never easy, she always had to work. She ran a small shop for some time but would end up as a solderer. Soldering, in those days, was a hot, smelly profession. Joining pieces of metal together with molten solder with a handheld soldering iron, heated on a hot flame. Burns were inevitable. As with everything else in her life, she took pride in her work, always committed to doing her best. She worked all through her life, returning to full-time work at age 67, after her years of looking after me were over.

Loss and tragedy could have blighted her life, but instead she rose to every challenge. After her mother died, she took on responsibility for her father. After her husband died, her two daughters became her sole responsibility too. Later, in 1946, she would lose her eldest

UNRELIABLE MEMORIES

daughter, my mother Mary, to cancer, and then I became another of her responsibilities. She never complained and loved us all, unconditionally.

In my childish memories she was ever-present. When I was two years old my mother contracted breast cancer and swiftly died. My father was, of course devastated, but Nan stepped in to make sure I was looked after. For the next seven years, she was there Monday to Friday. There when I woke up, and she would put me to bed at night. After Dad got home from work, she would go back to the house she shared with her remaining daughter, Lily and her two children, Eunice and Janet. Lily was by this time also a widow.

She continued to work as a solderer through most of those years, doing what was known as 'out-work.' Once a week a delivery of parts to solder would be delivered to her council house in Oakcroft Road, Nan would solder them together working in her kitchen, heating the irons on the gas stove, and the completed product would be collected the next week. Nan was paid 'piecework,' a fixed rate for each completed item. I can still remember the acrid smell of the flux in the kitchen and the piles of tin ware.

She had a good relationship with Grandma Kesseler and would often take me to visit as a young boy. The number 11 bus to 'The Yew Tree' and then the 16 to Whittington Oval. On the way she would admonish me to be on my best behaviour because, "Your Grandma is a lady". Lady was a title that she would never have aspired to although her background in Deritend was little different to Winnies. What she was, though, was a carer. Not just to me but to everyone around. For example, when war broke out in 1939 my great-aunt, Dora (Winnie's sister) and her husband Ayl were stuck in India. Their boys, Kenneth and Alan were at a services boarding school but, with their parents overseas, they had nowhere to go in the school holidays. These boys had no relationship with Jinnie but that made no difference. She made them a part of the extended family. Ken never forgot that.

If there was a death in Oakcroft Road, it was Mrs. Deffley who would lay out the corpse. She fulfilled the position of "wise woman" in that street. She mothered us all and she helped bring up her two granddaughters as well as me.

The last couple of years of her life were plagued with illness and the need for a colostomy bag, with which she felt uncomfortable and embarrassed. She died in Selly Oak hospital in early 1967 with me and my cousin Janet at her side. Her last words before she slipped away that night were, "Don't bother Lizzie with this tonight". We didn't, we passed on the news to her sister the following morning. Her selflessness still leaves me amazed. She was the one that made sure that although I may not have had a mom, I was never short of love, Nan and the other females in my family made sure of that.

.

CHAPTER 3 – DAD AND MOM

My father was born on 28th February 1907, the third son. He spent his early years in Deritend, attending Floodgate Street School. He was close to both of his elder brothers but especially to Syd. They shared a love of scouting and there is a memorial to them both at Gilwell Park which was and is the Scouts HQ in Essex. This is part of the Scouts Promise Path initiative and was sponsored by Syd's son, Michael. It is probably the only one there dedicated to brothers. Scouting was very important to both of them, and I remember Dad taking me to the 9th World Scout Jamboree, also known as the Jubilee Jamboree, which was held at Sutton Park for twelve days during August 1957. He talked fondly about those days in the St. Gabriel's Troop with Syd.

Another of Ted's passions was football. **FAMILY STORY ALERT.** I was always led to believe that he was on the books at Birmingham City as a young man. He never reached the first team, finally giving up football after an injury during a match against Walsall reserves. His claim to fame was playing alongside the legendary Blues centre forward, Joe Bradford. Apocryphal or not, I can confirm that he was on good terms with Joe Bradford, who, in my young years, ran a café near to St. Andrews, the Blues ground. When we went there Joe would greet Ted warmly. So, who knows?

I don't know when or how he met Mary Deffley, but they lived relatively close to each other. They were married at St. Gabriel's on 2nd August 1930. Ted was 22 and Mary was 20. At 20 you were not then allowed to make decisions for yourself, especially when it came to consent to marriage. If you were to be married young you had to get your parents' permission. This usually meant the boy asking the girl's father for her hand in marriage. However, Mary's father was dead by this time and Ted was told to ask her grandfather, John Cooper. **FAMILY STORY ALERT.** Apparently, Ted feared Mr. Cooper and could not summon the courage to ask the question. So, he asked his father, Joe, to speak to Mr. Cooper on his behalf. He did, they got on like a house on fire and the marriage went ahead.

Mary was a dressmaker and seamstress working at the Beehive store in Birmingham City Centre. Ted was an engineer, a profession that stayed on his passport through the rest of his life. They both wanted children, but Mary had a series of miscarriages and they resigned themselves to not having a family.

At the start of the Second World War, they were living in rented accommodation at 318 Yardley Wood Road, in the Yardley Wood District of Birmingham. Ted was working in a reserved occupation at the BSA and was, therefore, not called up for military duty. The position at BSA didn't last long, however. **FAMILY STORY ALERT.** The story goes that one of the night-time supervisors, on Dad's shift, was abusing his position with sexual approaches to the girls under his control. One night this got out of hand with one of the girls in tears. Ted challenged the supervisor and, getting nowhere with that approach, laid him out. Of course, in normal times, this would be a sacking offence, but these weren't normal times. It was very difficult to dismiss someone from a reserved occupation, but something would have to be done. Ted was transferred to another position in Coventry at the Standard Aero No. 1 Factory. This was a 'shadow' factory built next to the Standard Motor factory to use the expertise in mass production to make the De Haviland Mosquito. He remained there for the rest of the war.

Coventry is approximately 20 miles away from Yardley Wood and with fuel restricted, blackout, and odd work patterns, it was not practical to travel back and forth every day, so he obtained digs in a pub close to the factory. He would travel back to Birmingham whenever he had a couple of days off.

Coventry was, of course, a prime target for the Luftwaffe and in

November 1940, Ted had a stroke of luck that possibly saved his life. He had two days off work and went home to Mary on Thursday 14th November. That night the Luftwaffe really unloaded on Coventry, the worst of the blitz so far. The pub that Ted was staying in was destroyed in that raid. Of course, nothing was allowed to stop the production and on Saturday, he was back at work.

Mary filled her time when not at work by making wedding dresses for friends and neighbours. With rationing in force these were made from everything available from parachute silk to remodelling old dresses. Apparently, she was in great demand.

In early 1944 Mary found that she was, again, pregnant. With her history, this must have been a worrying time. However, this time, she carried the baby to term and on 23rd August 1944, I was born in Loveday Street Maternity Hospital.

FAMILY STORY ALERT. I have already mentioned my great-aunt Dora and her husband Ayl. The month before my birth they had finally got back to the UK from India. Ayl continued his RAF service and Dora started to make a home for her and her boys in Hawarden in North Wales. On the 24th of August they were visiting Winnie, Dora's sister, in Birmingham and decided to come and see the new child in hospital. In those days the Matron was the authority in hospitals and the rule in the Maternity hospital was that only fathers could visit. The Hollands were, of course, refused permission. The Matron was called, and Dora told her that she should be ashamed to deny Squadron Leader Holland permission to see his only great-nephew before he returned to active service with all the risks that that involved. Suitably chastened, Matron used her discretion and allowed a short visit. The truth was that Ayl was now being transferred to a desk job with the United States Air Force at their base at Hawarden. His biggest danger was over-eating on American rations!

After 14 years of marriage, Ted and Mary were delighted to finally be parents and no doubt looked forward to a lifetime together. Sadly, that was not to be.

The war ended and Ted was able to leave Standard Aero and return to work in Birmingham. He started his own little engineering business and was doing quite well before disaster struck. In late 1946 Mary was diagnosed with breast cancer. In those pre-NHS days. Surgery was expensive. Ted sold everything, including his business, to fund the treatment. Everything failed and on 22nd May 1947, Mary died. Understandably, Ted was devastated. He had lost his beloved wife; he had no income, and he had a 20-month-old son to look after. Those around him told me later that they feared that the pressure would be too much for him. I have no doubt that, in his grief, he was on the verge of a nervous breakdown.

FAMILY STORY ALERT. In fact, so worried were the members of his family about his ability to bring up the baby that his sister, my lovely Aunt Ruth, looked at the possibility of adopting me, to ensure that I was brought up in the family.

At this point, two things happened. Firstly, my Nan, stepped in to take over child-care in the way that I have previously described. Secondly, Dad got the offer of a position with Bank & Davis Limited, in River Street, Deritend.

Banks & Davis had, fairly obviously, been founded many years before by Henry Davis and his partner Mr. Banks. The Banks part of the partnership left pre-war, but the company had a 'good' war. They had made their trade making holloware fittings, mainly handles for cookware. Changing over the press works to the war effort was easy and they produced billycans, field kitchen equipment as well as continuing to supply handles to other manufacturers. The early days of the war proved especially beneficial for the company. Whenever the British Army retreated it was important to bring with them their weapons, but kitchen equipment was not so important. This provided a rich order book for replacements. By the end of the war the company was profitable and, therefore, saleable. Henry Davis decided to sell.

Of course, after the conflict had ended, the orders dropped off and the new owners were faced with a company whose production was going down and costs were going up. They were looking for a manager who could trim the costs and return the business to profit. Ted Kesseler was given a six-month contract, to be renewed if he was successful.

He put everything into the job, six days a week. Able to do so because I was being looked after by Nan, he poured his skill, enthusiasm, and effort into turning the business round. He met all of the targets set him and, with the first successful six months behind him, he started planning for his long-term future.

So, another chapter of his life began as an ambitious businessman, determined to make a better life for himself and his family.

CHAPTER 4 – EARLY YEARS IN YARDLEY WOOD.

Our little house at 318 Yardley Wood Road had two bedrooms and a bathroom upstairs, a living room, kitchen and a 'front room' downstairs. The front room was almost never used, kept for best and the occasional visitor. Looking back, I can never remember the bathroom being used either!

Next door, on the corner of Windemere Road, was the Post Office and corner shop run by Mrs. Whitehouse. Opposite was a Road Roller Depot and a large pig farm. I remember being invited to the pig farmer's daughter's birthday party when I was about five or six. They were well off, if slightly smelly, and had a conjuror to entertain the kids. I was fascinated and retain my interest in stage magic to this day.

My childhood memories are all happy ones. 'How can that be?', I hear you cry, 'Your mother died when you were two!'. That is, in fact, the point. I was so young that I have no memories of Mary, although a lot of stories implanted by my relatives. The pain of loss was certainly felt by Dad and Nan, but for me those early years were idyllic. Summer days playing with my cousin Janet 'down the Dingles', the place where the River Cole crossed Brook Lane, just a short walk from Nan's house. Fishing for frog spawn down the Dell, now known nationally as Moseley Bog. Playing in Swanshurst Park around the pool which was made in c. 1759 by Henry Giles as a fishing pond. In 2024 you can still see brave fishermen sat by the side of the pool in all weathers. I remember my pastimes, in summer the sun always shone and, of course, it snowed in winter. The truth is that it probably wasn't like that, but this is how I remember it.

Holidays were always important in our family. Actually, my first memories are of a holiday and is also a reminder of the title of this journal.

In the late spring of 1946, dad, Mary my mother, Nan and I had a week's holiday in Hastings, Sussex. We drove there in my dad's little car which was, in fact, two half cars welded together during the war and which my dad drove until he bought CNP 683 when I was four.

On the way to Sussex, we had two punctures. With only one spare, dad had to repair the inner tube on the tyre and reinflate it with a foot pump.

I also clearly remember a walk during this holiday, when dad, carrying me in his arms, stumbled while crossing a stream and, desperate that I shouldn't fall in the water, tossed me gently into a patch of lush grass on the nearby bank. The greenery he dropped me into turned out not to be grass but nettles. Luckily, I was well wrapped up.

Of the foregoing three paragraphs, only the first, about the car, is undeniably true. The other two are definitely "Unreliable Memories" or, more accurately, "Implanted Memories". I believed them to be true into my late teens when I realised that they couldn't be. At the time of that holiday, I would be less than two years old, and I know now that I have no true recollections of my mother. What I do have is the stories that others later shared with me, and I took on as my truth. It makes me wonder what early years stories I hear from my friends are as insubstantial as mine.

My cousins, Janet, and Eunice, lived with their mom, my Aunt Lil at Nan's house. Janet was a couple of years older than me and would play with me, while Eunice was far too old to bother with a snotty nosed kid like me. In the summer months I would spend much of my time in Oakcroft Road, playing with the other kids in the street. Football, marlies, Mr. Wolf, skipping games (I could never skip) all played on the roadway or, as my Nan would call it, the horse-road. Horses there were, the milk float and the coal truck pulled by great carthorses. My job, when the coal man delivered, was to count the

15

sacks as they came through the house and into the 'coal-hole' in the kitchen. Each sack was a hundredweight, and 20 sacks made a ton.

The freedom we had as children would amaze my grandchildren now. We would go off, sometimes with bottles of water and bread and butter, in the morning and come back for tea. If feeling adventurous, we would walk to Trittiford Park which had a large pond with an island in the middle and could be reached by walking alongside the River Cole from Brook Lane. We would play at cowboys and Indians or swing from rope swings across the river. This once ended with me stranded halfway across dangling over the water. Having realised there was nothing she could do, Janet left me hanging there and went home. Eventually I let go of the rope and dropped into the water, no more than a foot deep. I don't remember who got into more trouble, me for being wet or Janet for leaving me.

For my fifth birthday, Big Lil, another aunt from my maternal side, bought me a puppy. A mainly brown mongrel, he was named Patch, because of the black patch over one eye. We already had a cat, Tiddles, who did not appreciate the new arrival at all. Tiddles was a hunting cat. She would go out at night and, the following morning, Nan would find a present on the back step comprising all Tiddles catches for the night. Daytime was her resting time, and she did not welcome this boisterous puppy who bothered her and interrupted her rest. She would snarl and spit at him and, eventually, he learned to keep his distance. That was until he got hit by a car on the Yardley Wood Road. Gentle reader, you must appreciate that these were different times, we would let our dogs out to roam freely and, most of the time they were safe. However, accidents did happen, and Patch got his leg badly broken. He was 'patched up' by the vet (see what I did there!) and returned home much the worse for wear and unable to get around. Tiddles attitude changed almost overnight, she seemed to sense his distress and would even push her food bowl over to him to share. They never fought again until the cat died in 1952.

I vaguely remember my first day at College Road Infants School. What I remember most is Nan leaving me and me bawling my eyes

UNRELIABLE MEMORIES

out. In the five years I was there I remember only two things, making friends with Ronald Coleman (yes, really his name!) who lived in a prefab in Coldbath Road, and the death of King George VI.

The death of the King was a profound moment in our nation's history, but to a 7-year-old it was notable for only two things. At that time there was a school's radio programme called 'Music and Movement' which was used to get children to take some exercise to music. It was a regular staple at College Road School and so, on the Wednesday, 6th February 1952, we trooped into the hall as usual. Just after the programme started, it was interrupted to announce the death of the King, that morning. The programme was taken off the air, replaced by solemn music, and we children returned to our classrooms. My second memory was seeing a teacher crying. Of course, at that age I had no idea how loved the King was and how important his leadership had been, especially through the bombing raids on the big cites.

Of course, his death meant a new Queen. His daughter, Elizabeth, was in Kenya on a state visit when her father died. A courier informed her husband, the Duke of Edinburgh, and he had the unenviable job of telling his wife that her beloved father had passed. They immediately returned to London, where she took the oath of succession. That meant a Coronation, certainly the biggest national event in my young life. Tuesday, 2nd June 1953 saw street parties across the city, including ours in Oakcroft Road. Tables laden with sandwiches, homemade cakes, jelly, and whatever treats families could donate. A free tin of chocolates, courtesy of Cadburys and a boom in the sales of televisions. For the first time cameras were allowed in Westminster Abbey and millions gathered around flickering, tiny, black and white screens to see the ceremony.

In our family, it was mu Nan's sister, Liz, who had the first TV. It was a Bakelite bodied Bush with, of course, just one channel, the BBC.

Though the TV was exciting, it wasn't until the following week when we visited the Tatler News Theatre in Station Street, that we experienced the opulence and glamour of the event in glorious colour. The Tatler, was a regular outing for me and my Nan. It showed cartoons, newsreels, and a serial. I remember watching Batman, Superman, Roy Rogers, and Gene Autry (both singing cowboys) and more. The Taler is now known at The Electric Cinema, the oldest working cinema in the country, but unfortunately in 2024 under threat

One thing that I must admit, in hindsight, was that I was terribly spoiled. Of course, I was, I was the little boy who had no mother. I did, however, have aunts, and they smothered me with kindness. Big Lil (Lily Hubbard) lived not far from Trittiford Park, and we would visit often. As her nickname would suggest, she was a large lady, with a heart as big as the bosoms that covered it. She had been very close to my mother, and it was at her house, 4 Selma Grove, that Mary passed away. **FAMILY STORY ALERT.** By the time of her passing, Mary was in a bad way, the cancer had progressed throughout her body and had progressed to her throat, meaning she was unable to speak. There are three bedrooms at 4 Selma Grove, with their doors meeting around a small, square, landing. Lil and her husband, Tubby, were in the from room, my father was in the larger back bedroom and my mom in the smaller bedroom at the back. Strangely, this was the room that I would later occupy after leaving home. I always felt comfortable there.

On the night she died, Lil and my dad came rushing from their rooms at the same time, because they had heard Mary cry out. When they entered her room, she had just passed. It was only later that they realised that they had only heard their own name called, and that physically Mary couldn't have called at all. Make of that what you will.

Another important Auntie was Nan's sister, Liz. Liz lived in Acocks Green with her husband Edgar. In my young days they kept chickens in their back garden, as they had done throughout the war. These were mainly for eggs but, if a hen stopped laying, there was no room for sentiment, it ended up in the pot. I vividly remember Uncle Edgar decapitating a chicken on the chopping block on the back yard. A bit gruesome, but a valuable reminder of where our food comes from.

Their daughter Vera was my godmother, and I would spend many happy hours playing with her daughter, Christine. Her husband, John (or Jack) Price, had been a paratrooper in the war, but was captured near Arnhem during Operation Market Garden. Like many ex-servicemen he rarely spoke about his experiences.

Like most Brummie families, our holidays were spent either at Rhyl in North Wales or in Weston-Super-Mare. My memories of Rhyl are very vague, but I remember the happy times we spent in Weston. We stayed in a bed and breakfast in the Uphill district run by Mrs. Valentine. It was always Dad, Nan, and I but I remember being joined by Little Lil (my mother's sister) and her girls, Janet, and Eunice. Mrs. Valentine seemed to have a soft spot for me, and I still recall her hot chocolate, the first time I can ever remember having it. Rumours surfaced later that she also had a soft spot for my dad, but I have no knowledge of that!

In these early years, there is one other holiday that stands out in my mind. Nan, Dad, and I went to spend two weeks on a working farm somewhere outside Stratford-upon-Avon. As was often the case with my father, he would stay for a couple of days and then 'have to' get back to the business. This holiday went so well that we ended up extending it for at least another week, memory tells me it could have been longer, but memory is unreliable! I do remember loving the life on the farm. I would go out into the henhouses and collect eggs, 'help' bring in the cows for milking, feed the pigs, remembering to not get between a large pig and the sty-wall, and generally busy myself around the farm. For a city boy this was an experience that has stayed with me throughout my life.

My mother's younger sister, Lil (known as Little Lil to distinguish her from Lily Hubbard) remains an enigma. I can never remember her working or having a job. She had been married to a man called George Mackmar. Already pregnant when she got married, her fist daughter, Eunice, was born in June 1939 followed by Janet on the 11th of December 1940.

George, who we think was born around 1904, joined the Army

during the war but was discharged on medical grounds and died from cancer on 24th March 1942. Those are the things I think are true about George, but I can verify none of it, except the date of his death. After much research, nobody in the family can locate any records of George, it is as if he never really existed.

Lil and her girls lived with my Nan at 78 Oakcroft Road, a council house that they moved into in 1939. It was a well build house in a quiet road in Billesley, just off the Yardley Wood Road and relatively close to where Dad and Mary were living. The front door led to the stair well with the stairs in front of you, and the door to the sitting room to your right. The sitting room was a decent size with an open coal fire. Leading from there was the kitchen which had, on the left, the 'coal-hole' for storing the fuel, and the pantry. The back door led out from the kitchen to a small garden with a door from the garden into the toilet. I believe that sometime after the house was built the Council revamped the toilet as a bathroom with an entrance from the kitchen. Upstairs there were three bedrooms. The front bedroom was Nans. If I stayed here overnight, that is where I would sleep, warm and safe with Nan by my side. In fact, I didn't have a bed of my own until I was nine, because at home I would share the bed with my dad.

Shopping was mainly done locally, at the butchers and grocery stores on the Yardley Wood Road. Sometimes we would go to the delights of Ladypool Road, then, as now, a melange of independently owned shops. There was a home-made ice-cream shop there that still lives in my memory. An excursion to Birmingham city-centre was known as 'going to town'. It was there that the big stores like The Beehive, Greys, C&A and Lewis's were situated. Lewis's was by far the largest with, I think, five floors. These were served, not only by lifts with attendants, but with the only wooden escalator that I can ever remember. Of course, to a young child this was not just a means of transport between floors, it was a plaything. One day I get on the escalator, full of excitement, not realising that Nan had not noticed. I soon did realise that I was along and lost. My wailing attracted help and a kindly shopgirl looked after me until Nan was found. She was so relieved to have got me back safely that she gave me a hefty slap for my pains.

Of course, the other annual reason for going to Lewis's was to see Father Christmas. This Father Christmas was obviously the real one. He even had a parade through the city on his sleigh when he was installed in the store. Because of this he was very popular. You would enter the store from the back door by The Minories (a little street that separated the two halves of the store) and queue up the five flights of stairs until you got to the toy department situated on the top floor. There you would be greeted by Uncle Holly and, in your turn, directed through the grotto to meet the jovial, white bearded man. Spoiler! What we didn't know then was that there were two Santa's and two grottos, this kept the crowd moving and no one was ever the wiser.

Christmas was big in the family. On Christmas Eve we would gather for a party, usually at Aunt Lizzies. There was a piano, old songs were sung, food and drink would be taken, and a good time was had by all. At some time during the evening, Father Christmas would make an appearance for the younger children. I remember one year being surprised to note that Santa had the same tattoos as Uncle Edgar.

Because Dad was working six days a week to fulfil his dream of someday owning Banks & Davis, he would feel guilty and shower me with expensive presents. I remember especially a huge wooden rocking horse and a pedal racing car that could have been the end of me. Windemere Road was a steep hill and I recall racing down it in my little car and then realising, as I approached the main Yardley Wood Road, that I was going too fast to stop or turn. Luckily, there was no traffic on the road, and I sailed safely across, stopping in the entrance to the pig farm. The other stand-out present was the 'silver' bike. What I didn't know was that dad had bought it second hand, had it taken apart and all the paintwork stripped and then every part was chromium plated at Banks and Davis. It gleamed and was my pride and joy, nobody else had a silver bike!

In retrospect, those years seemed endless, but passed all too quickly.

As I approached my ninth birthday, the world was about to change for me.

CHAPTER 5 - TED AND MAISIE

The truth is I don't know where or when, Dad met the woman who was to become my stepmother. My sister Barbara says that it was in a pub in Digbeth, but she wasn't there either!

Maisie Lee was the daughter of Ada and Ernest Lee. She had one older brother, Cyril and two younger ones, Fred, and Leslie. They all lived at 42 Ninfield Road, Acocks Green where the garden backed onto the railway line. She was born on 13th April 1927.

I don't believe that I can remember Maisie before she was engaged to my dad, but obviously they had been 'courting' for some time before I was informed. I do, however, have vivid memories of her grandmother, Ada Roper. Mrs. Roper ran a little general store on Digbeth High Street. She was a fierce, strong woman, which I guess that you needed to be to run an independent shop in those days.

Thursday night was faggots and peas night. Come 6pm a queue would be forming down to the side entrance where Ada and her son George would dole out home-made faggots and peas into the bowls and basins that their customers would bring. Apart from the fish and chip shops, this was the first take-away food I had ever come across. And it was delicious! To this day I have never found faggots that approach the taste I remember from 'Old girl Roper'. She ran a very tight ship, and the family story is that she frightened away every girlfriend George ever had, because she needed him in the shop. George never married.

Her daughter, also named Ada, married Ernest Lee at St. John's, Deritend on 21st April 1924. The marriage certificate records her as being 19, but she was only 17 having been born in January 1907. I must assume the wedding had been brought forward because Cyril was born in October 1924. Following Maisie in 1927, Fred was born in 1929 and Les, the afterthought, in 1941. Ada Lee was a large, very buxom, lady. As a boy, a cuddle from Mrs. Lee could easily lead to suffocation.

Her husband, Ernie, was a lovely man. I only remember him as a sickly man, sitting in the corner of the living room, occasionally coughing. He had been a paint and varnish mixer and the fumes had affected his lungs. He died in 1964 from Acute and Chronic Bronchitis.

I suppose that I must have been nervous about the coming marriage because I do remember family re-assuring me before the wedding that everything would be fine, after all, I was getting a new mother. The wedding took place at St. Mary's, Acocks Green in May 1953. The groom was 20 years older than his attractive young wife. My sole memory of the day is 'helping' at the bar at the reception! At the end of the evening, the bride and groom went off to their honeymoon and, as arranged, I went to stay with my Aunt Ruth and Uncle Tom for the fortnight that Mom and Dad were away. (I started calling Maisie 'Mom' straight away. I don't remember that as being strange, I had never used the word before!).

In fact, they didn't go away at all! Mom wasn't feeling too well after the reception so, instead of the seaside, they moved into their new house at 48 Farnol Road, Yardley two weeks early. Mom must have recovered pretty soon, for just 9 months later, my sister, Barbara, arrived. I should point out that Aunt Ruth's house was in the next road from our new house, but none of us knew that the newlyweds were that close.

The 'honeymoon' over, it was time for me, and Patch the dog, to move into the new family home. 48 Farnol Road is a three bedroomed house with two rooms and a kitchen on the ground floor. It had a large back garden with a garage which was approached by a drive that curled behind the houses. Unlike 318 Yardley Wood Road, it was modern, light and had a functional hot water system!

I was allocated the small front bedroom. This was the first big change, for I had never had a room of my own. I had always shared with Dad and, at first, I didn't like it. But that passed. There were many other changes, of course. Being part of a new, and growing, family. A new school, where I knew no-one, and a new GP. The new GP brought more changes. For as long as I can remember, I had suffered with asthma. Originally diagnosed by our family doctor when I was three, it meant that I was a 'sickly' child. Often unable to run around and play with the other kids. There was no medication for the problem, so I just had to get on with it.

My new GP had a new thought. The major problem that children had with asthma was that an attack, with the feeling that the air was being dragged out of you and you were unable to breathe in, would often be accompanied with panic attacks. The panic, of course, made the asthma worse. A vicious cycle. So, he decided that I should be referred to the Children's Hospital, in Birmingham. There still was no medication so the treatment consisted of breathing exercises designed to give you the ability to control an attack without going into panic. This was two afternoons every week for the whole of the last school year at Yardley School, seriously disrupting my schooling. It did have beneficial effects and I was, thereafter, able to control all but the worst asthma attacks.

Those of us in the clinic knew that the really ill young patients were sent to Davos in the mountains of Switzerland, where they could benefit from the altitude and clean air. They would be sent off for a month. Of course, at the end of that they would return to the highly polluted atmosphere of Birmingham! I was glad not to have been recommended for this, the thought of a month away from home and family was scary. This treatment in Switzerland was made possible by the confectioner, Christian Kunzel, whose cakeshop Nan and I would go to as a special treat. The speciality was a milk chocolate cup filled with cake. Wicked but delicious.

Kunzel had been born in Davos and moved to Birmingham in 1903, after spending time as a chef at the House of Commons. He opened a bakery in Snow Hill and the café and shop in Midland Arcade. In 1932 he was elected Chair of the Children's Hospital and thereafter opened his family home in Davos to some patients. The hospital maintained a small staff there paid for by the kindness of the compassionate confectioner.

In the summer of 1953, we went on our first holiday as a family. Two weeks in Ireland, the first time I had ever been out of the UK. It was a first for Nan, who was brought along, I believe, to provide some extra stability for me and allow Dad and Mom some private time. The boat trip across the Irish Sea was horrendous. Unless you had booked a private cabin, below decks were only sitting rooms/dormitories for men and women. Nan, who had never been on a boat before, went straight into the women's quarters. Leaving me with Mom and Dad. As the sea began to get heavy, Mom excused herself and went below.

Around us were scenes of carnage, the sea got rougher, the passengers got sicker. Dad, who always prided himself on being a 'good sailor' eventually succumbed and had to get someone to go and find Nan to look after me. The old lady was found and joined me on deck. We both seemed to be quite immune to the vomit inducing swell and quite enjoyed the rest of our voyage.

Mom's best friend, Evelyn, was married to a charismatic young Irishman, Al Raitt, and, although I can't be sure, I think that we spent the first week of the holiday lodging at their house in Dublin. I remember Nan getting on well with Al's mother. His brother had a sports car and I remember being whizzed around as a special treat in that.

The second week we spent in a B&B in the East coast seaside town of Bray. My memories are of an attractive resort, but on a return visit a few years ago, I found it to be a grey town on a grey coastline. Had it changed? Or is my childhood memory inaccurate?

Back home, I was settling into a new routine. School was Church Road Junior, just past the Yew Tree in Yardley. This was a short bus ride with the bus stop at the top of the road. Although, as the new boy in a group that had been together since Infant School, establishing myself was difficult. Eventually I did manage to make some new friends and enjoyed school, although I was definitely not academic.

I spent time with my cousin, Jean, helped by the fact that there was a passageway from almost opposite our house through to Vibart Road. I also was becoming quite content with my own company, happy to play alone and read. Reading would become a passion.

Encouraged by Aunt Ruth, I started attending Yardley Parish Church, St. Edburgha's. The vicar there was Canon Charles Crowson, and he was a likeable and approachable cleric. My churchgoing habit pleased my Grandma, and, on many Sundays, I would catch the bus to have lunch with her and Granddad. Sometimes I would be asked questions about the service just to make sure I had been attending!

As I said earlier, baby Barbara arrived on 6th January 1954, changing the family dynamic. Mom, who was trying hard to learn how to cope with me, now had a baby of her own to deal with. If there had been a joint in my nose, it would have been put out! With all the benefits of hindsight, I can now see that Maisie was doing her best. I can't have been easy for her. If my life had been upended, then so had hers. Her husband was still a workaholic, now working hard to establish a new part of the business, and she was left alone for a great deal of the time. Like most married women of the time, she had given up working when she married and now, with a baby, there was no chance of going back. That meant that another source of companionship was gone, and she had to get on with this new, challenging, life.

Banks & Davis was beginning to flourish, and Dad was made Managing Director. The company had been sold again and the majority stockholding was now with a Mr. Young. At the time of the sale Dad had taken the opportunity to buy some shares for himself. Although this stretched his finances, it was to prove an invaluable move in the future. Banks & Davis's core business was described as 'holloware fittings'. What this meant in practise was that they made handles for pots and pans, buckets, and bins. They also did contract presswork for other companies and had both hand-presses (also known as fly-presses) and power-presses. The main power press shop, in River Street, Deritend, was full of the noise of machines pounding pieces of sheet steel into various shapes. In 1954, all the presses were run from a central engine via an elaborate system of belts and wheels. One long axle ran above the workshop, turned by the engine, and from that axle great leather belts ran to the individual presses, turning their flywheels. Occasional the belts would snap, and lethal chunks of heavy leather would fly across the plant. Health and Safety were nowhere in sight.

By this time that central engine was diesel powered but, up until the late 1940's, there was a steam engine which drew its water from a well situated at the side if the press shop. As I remember it from the 1950's the building ran from 43-67 River Street. On the ground floor was the Managing Directors Office, with his secretary's office next door, the guillotine shop and sheet metal store on the street front. Behind that was the power press shop, and to the left of it the hand (or fly) press shop. This also held the chrome plating plant. The first thing that hit you when you entered this part of the building was the stench of chemicals. Above that. On the first floor, was the larger hand press shop, connected by a staircase and a rickety goods lift.

The factory was on the banks of Birmingham's premier river, the River Rea, which runs along a brick culvert at the back of the building. Some of the chrome and brass items that were manufactured had to be polished, and the polishing shop was on an extension that went over the river. Obviously, it was called The Bridge.

The entrance to the offices were through a door on River Street and were on the first floor, as was the warehouse where goods were packed and stored. The office was run by Mrs. Betty Hopkins, a wise and resourceful woman. That main office also housed the General Manager, Jimmy Cain, who did most of the customer liaison and had been there throughout the war. I remember being fascinated by the switchboard, an array of plugs and cables by which you could physically connect incoming calls to the extension phones throughout the building. The switchboard operator, usually also the office junior, would answer calls with "Victoria 2988, Banks & Davis, can I help you?"

In 1954, the business was about to change substantially. The main trade fair was the British Industries Fair (The BIF), held at Castle Bromwich on the outskirts of the city. It was on the site of the Castle Bromwich aerodrome, used during the ward for ferrying planes out to the stations across the country.

Hundreds of companies would have stands there, advertising their products and services and looking for new customers from all over the world. This was the company listing in the catalogue for that year.

"Banks & Davis, Limited. Stand A510. River Street, Deritend, Birmingham, 5. Telephone. Victoria 2988. Tel. Add.: " Seamless, Birmingham."-Manufacturers all types Holloware Fittings, Handles for Saucepans, Kettles, Maslins, Buckets, Milkchurns, etc. Largest Trade Suppliers of Fittings for Aluminium, Enamel and Galvanised Ware, Stompers and Pressworkers, Tinsmiths' and Coppersmiths' Fittings."

The fair ran for 10 days and, on one of those days, I accompanied my dad to the stand. Normally he would walk around with me as I would take in the various displays which ranged from heavy industry to toy manufacturers and housewares. This year, however, a foreign visitor turned up, and I was handed over to a young office worker, Beryl, brought in to look after the stand. Instead of greeting people she found herself baby-sitting the Managing Director's son.

The visitor was Josef Blum from a company called Leifheit, in Soligen, Germany. They had patented a sponge mop with a special hardwearing sponge and a unique wringing action, and they were looking for a company who could manufacture and market in the UK. Dad saw an opportunity to diversify and, over the next year, put in a great effort to persuade Herr Blum that Banks & Davis were the partners that they were looking for.

He was successful and in 1956 an agreement was signed, and the 'Ato-Mop' was launched. A British chemical company was approached to manufacture the PVA sponge, and aluminium castings were sourced, and a new manufacturing shop was put into the River Street premises. Later I will explain how this made the business much more profitable and secured the family finance, although not before a major scare.

In March 1955, the family grew with the birth of Edward Macdonald Kesseler and, with Barbara being only 15 months old, Mom had her work cut out.

Back at school I was entered for the 11+ examinations. Birmingham had a flourishing Grammar School system and entry to these selective schools was by examination. You, or your parents, listed the schools that you would like to go to, in preferential order. Dad decided that Camp Hill Grammar School for Boys, would be the best for me, so that became first choice. Of course, I was not expected to pass the exam, my schooling had been interrupted by my visits to the Children's Hospital, but we were all expected to take it, so I did.

Results were posted out on postcards, and, to my surprise, I passed and got my first preference. I probably skipped to school that day to share the good news. The post was reliable in those days and most of us got our results on the same morning. However, the teacher was not impressed by my assurances that I had passed. So certain that I was making up the story were they that I was sent home to bring the postcard as proof! To be fair, they may have had some reason, I believe my imagination was active at 10.

But passed I had. Not, in my opinion, because I was academically clever, but because I was good at intelligence tests and that was what the 11+ basically was. I was off to Camp Hill, another new school where I would know no-one, but that would be the same as many of my peers. I was approaching 11 and the next phase of my life.

CHAPTER 6 - SECONDARY SCHOOL YEARS.

Looking back over a long life the change from junior school to a selective Grammar School rates as one of the great culture changes. King Edward VI Camp Hill Grammar School for Boys, to give it its full title, started educating boys in September 1883, so by the time I entered the school buildings were 72 years old, and showing their age. The footsteps of generations of boys had worn curves into the stone staircase.

As part of the King Edwards Foundation, it was also a school steeped in traditions. Emulating Public Schools, we had Houses, and I was placed into Seymour House. House points could be scored for academic and sporting prowess. In five years, I never earned a point! The school played Rugby, Cricket, and Eton Fives. Of course, we had a uniform including a cap that everybody hated wearing.

The school building was on the Stratford Road, at Camp Hill. For me that meant one bus ride, on the 15b, and a walk up the hill from Digbeth High Street, On the way, I would often call into the baker's shop and buy a penny bun for my lunch snack. The main school tradition seemed to be bullying of the new kids. They were known as 'sherrings', possibly a diminution of 'fresh herrings'. In the playground was a metal staircase that used to be a fire escape from the basement woodwork room. By 1955 it was unused, and the bottom was full of water. The stairs had one or two steps broken and all were slippery. If a sherring annoyed a senior boy, he would be thrown down the 'Monkey Hole' as it was known. Even if you managed to keep your feet, the water would be waiting for you, but most would end up spreadeagled in the mucky liquid. Of course, nobody complained, it wasn't done to sneak.

There were three entry forms, allocated by age. 1S were the older boys (senior) 1M were the middle and I, born in late August, was in 1J (junior). I was, of course, only just 11 that September and there was only one boy younger in my year. I was also small, thin and, because of my history of asthma, not athletic. Rugby was especially fearsome. I spent most of my time when on the field, just trying to keep out of the way.

Academically I also struggled. Although I was adequate in English, Maths and Science, other subjects I found difficult. History, Geography, and the practical subjects like Woodwork I never got to grips with. Religious Education was a subject that I should have been good at, but the head of RE, Mr. Brown, was appalling. Of all the teachers I had over five years at Camp Hill, he was the worst, with his constant belittling of students he was probably the reason that many people were put off from Christianity!

The other major difference between secondary school and primary school was the dreaded homework. There was set tasks for every night and weekends, and all were marked. I must admit that I didn't take to this imposition and my results mirrored my lake of application. At the end of the school year, we were allocated our forms for the next year. The top third went into Form 2L, where Latin was added to their curriculum, the next third went to 2G, where they studied German. I was put into 2R. The 'R' did not stand for Russian! We all believed it meant 'Reject', and most of us lived up to it!

In the summer holidays in 1956, the Kesseler family moved house again. This time we moved into a lovely bungalow at 66 Horseshoes Lane, Sheldon. Three bedrooms, with a large living room that looked out at a garden that extended a long way where it met an area of waste ground that eventually became part of Sheldon Country Park. However, in 1956, it was a jungle with a small river running through it.

Of course, for me, this meant another disruption. I left behind my cousins, Jean, and Anne, and had to find new friends and new activities. I started to attend St. Giles Church in Sheldon, within walking distance of home and quickly settled into their youth setup. I also had made friends with two fellow pupils at Camp Hill who also lived in Sheldon. Dave Johns was a studious and serious boy and Dave Taylor was always good company. Dave Johns would remain a friend until his untimely death, and Dave Taylor remains my best friend until this day.

This was a year of changes. As well as the house move, the school moved. Camp Hill Boys school re-located to new school buildings in Vicarage Road, Kings Heath, for the start of the September 1956 term. The new school was spacious, with many modern facilities that the old school lacked. However, the journey there was longer and more complicated. A 58 or 60 bus to the Swan, Yardley, and then the number 11, Outer Circle, bus to Kings Heath. Total journey time an hour. I would use this time to catch up on the homework I hadn't done and to read the Daily Mirror! I was already interested in the wider world and the Mirror, at that time, was a serious left-wing newspaper with some excellent writers. It was also small enough to read on the bus!

I continued to struggle academically, usually finishing in the bottom three or four of the form. It was, at this time, however, that a couple of teachers began to make their mark on me. 'Polly' Bates was head of Mathematics and an imposing, traditional teacher. He would sweep into a room in his scholastic gown, trailing chalk dust. A disciplinarian, but with a grasp of his subject and an ability to impart that to his pupils. He made me realise that mathematics was interesting and useful.

The other was a young teacher, John Cleake. He taught English and can take credit for my ongoing love of theatre and, especially, Shakespeare. He introduced us to the Shakespearean plays by, firstly, telling us the story in his own words. This gave us a great start, which was then amplified on by playing us sections of the play from Long Playing records. Thus, we got to hear the bard's words spoken by Olivier, Gielgud, Ashcroft, and others. This brought the verse to life and, for me, was a revelation. I was, by now, going to the theatre regularly, but not to see plays. Round the corner from my father's business was a pub that he frequented. The White Swan, in Floodgate Street, was run by two maiden ladies who had, at one time, been variety performers. They often had artistes who were on the bill at the Birmingham Hippodrome staying with them. They also had free tickets for the first performance of the weekly variety show. This became my regular Wednesday evening treat. On my own, at age 11, I would go to the theatre on Broad Street, for the 6:15pm show. I would sit in the 'Imperial Fauteuils' (a French word meaning armchair, but a posh word for the Stalls!) and see some of the great stars coming towards the end of the careers and some new acts on the way up.

Variety was, just as it suggests, a range of different acts. The show would start with a dance act, and may feature jugglers, acrobats, magic acts and, of course, comedians and vocalists. There were so-called 'speciality' acts. I remember well seeing Roy Rogers, the movie cowboy, who sang pretty well. He was supported by his wife, Dale Evans, and his horse, Trigger. Trigger had his own act and would make his entrance through the auditorium and onto the stage.

It was the comedians that made the most impression. Norman Evans with his 'Over the Garden Wall' act in drag as a gossipy old lady, an up-and-coming double act called Morecambe and Wise and the best of them all, the great Jimmy Wheeler whose surreal comedy was way ahead of his time.

When the early show finished, the audience for the second performance was already queuing up at the front of the theatre, so we had to exit by the doors on the side. So, immediately the last notes of 'God save the Queen' had faded, the ushers would bellow, "Side exits only, side exits only" and we would shuffle out into the night and, for me, the number 58 bus home.

My love of 'legitimate' theatre really began in 1957. Mr. Cleake had arranged a school trip to the Birmingham Repertory Theatre (now known as 'The Old Rep') to see Shakespeare's 'Henry V'. The star was a young actor called Albert Finney and his way with the words, his stage presence and the whole ambience of the storytelling hooked me, and it has never let me go. Realising this, Mr. Cleake, arranged for me to benefit from a little-known bursary which paid for boys to go to the theatre. I had to make a small contribution, and, for that, I got to go to the Rep and to the Alexandra Theatre which also had a repertory company in the season.

I saw everything that I could from the classics to the modern. One new play that I still remember was Willis Hall's, 'The Long and the short and the tall'. Set in a little cabin in Malaya during the Second World War it was both gritty and gripping and, even to this day, the best anti-war play I have ever seen. My young mind was being assailed, moulded, and educated.

Time at school, however, was generally not enjoyable. The bullying and casual violence was, obviously, worse for those who were smaller, weaker or, even, less bright. I skipped school whenever I could. Often deciding at the last minute, I would stay on the 58 bus into town, instead of changing at the Swan. Once there I would spend my day in the library or at the cinema. The picture house of choice was the Scala in Smallbrook Street, a beautiful old cinema, but its appeal to me was that it opened in the morning, and I could hide there in the dark for most of the day.

I got very skilled at writing 'excuse' notes from Mom. Her signature was far easier to forge than Dads with its flamboyance swirls. I was sometimes found out and a parent would be summoned, and I would promise that it would never happen again. Of course, it did. Nobody ever tried to find out why I was unhappy at school.

After Barbara, Eddie and Jon were born family holidays took a different turn and Butlins became a venue of choice. I remember Clacton, Bognor, Pwllheli, and Skegness pretty clearly. On some of those holidays we were accompanied by Ada and Ernie Lee. My unreliable memory tells me that we were in Skegness in 1957 and I saw Cliff Richard and The Drifters in the Rock 'n' Roll Ballroom. The Drifters, of course, would change their name to The Shadows later.

As a 13-year-old, I remember being annoyed at having to "look after" my siblings, but in later years I realised I revelled in the

35

independence that Butlins gave me. Because it was an enclosed site, my parents were happy for me to go off on my own, as long as I met them for meals. Meals were part of the "all in" deal and were taken in huge, hangar-like, dining rooms with jolly redcoats making sure that we were enjoying ourselves. That said, the three course meals were substantial and at least as good as Mom's cooking!

I would usually go to the theatre at night. Normally the production would be a variety bill, sometimes with a visiting star. The standard was pretty good and Butlins would feature again, in later holidays, both on my own and with my own family. The only other holiday of note from these family holidays is the one that dad and I had in Weymouth. It wasn't planned to be a father and eldest son holiday but to understand why turned out that way you need to know a little about dad and Mom's relationship. At this time dad was working very hard to make Banks and Davis work. He was tetchy and sometimes ill-tempered which could lead to arguments at home.

The trait of Mom that riled him the most was her timekeeping, or rather the lack of it. She was late for everything, meaning that much was done last minute. Meals would be late, appointments missed, meetings delayed. It drove dad insane.

So, this particular Saturday morning, we were all due to go to Weymouth. However, mom was not ready, the kids were not ready. Dad and I were ready, however, so, when his patience finally shattered, I found myself bundled into the car and we went off on our own leaving the rest of the family behind. I cannot comprehend what kind of reception he got when we came home, I probably hid in my bedroom to avoid it. Looking back, it was cruel, especially on the kids but the old man could only take so much. This wasn't the only time this kind of thing happened, either. Years later at the end of a business trip/holiday in Germany, mom wasn't ready when the car came to take them to the airport. Dad left without her. She caught a later flight.

As school life went on, I began to concentrate my efforts on the subjects that I enjoyed, Mathematics, English Language and

Literature and General Science. These were the ones that I would do homework for, and my results were good. The other subjects held little interest for me and I, effectively, abandoned them. Of course, the teachers had an effect. I didn't like history, but the teacher, Geoff Saunders, was one of those who went the extra mile to make his subject interesting. On the other hand, the PE teacher fulfilled, for me at least, the role of sadist supreme. Firstly, I annoyed him for my lack of athletic ability. This man, who went on to coach British swimmers, failed completely to teach me to swim! His disdain bordered on cruelty, not just to me, but to all those too weak, fat, or ill to excel physically.

Then came the fourth year when he took over teaching us French. As bad as he was as getting me fit, he was worse at teaching a language. That was the year when I completely stopped doing his homework. As a punishment, he would beat me with a gym shoe. It seemed like a decent trade to me; I didn't waste time doing hated homework and he got his pleasure in beating a boy. Am I now bitter about it? Yes, people like him should never be allowed near children.

When I was 13, the situation at Banks & Davis changed in a way that was to affect our family for decades to come. Dad was a minority shareholder and Managing Director. He ran the company, and the company was profitable. The majority shareholder was, basically, a sleeping partner happy to leave the business in Dad's hands and take the dividend. Unfortunately, he died and left the majority shareholding to his son who I can only describe as devious. He wanted to sell, and it was made clear that the new buyers would put in their own management and Dad would be out of work.

He was so worried by this that he started to set up a small toolmaking business in rented property, just in case. The only possible good outcome was because of a clause in the Articles of Association of the company that said that before shares were sold to an outside person they must be offered, at a fair price, to other shareholders. The only other shareholder was Dad, but he did not have the funds to buy. The seller suspected that and was, therefore, confident that his sale would go through.

Dad looked at every possibility. He re-mortgaged the house in Horseshoes Lane, sold whatever he could but there was no way he could raise enough. He was, however, as devious as the seller. The problem was simple, he had to buy the available shares outright and personally. Although he didn't have the money, he did have a good reputation. He managed to persuade a friend to transfer the necessary funds into his bank, without any guarantees, but only on the morning that the final board meeting to agree the sale. One of the reasons for the timing of the transfer was that he was suspicious that the bank manager at the branch where the company banked, and Ted Kesseler also banked, was feeding information about his finances to the majority share owner.

The board meeting took place, and the sellers lawyer made the official offer to my father, which he accepted to the amazement of all. The seller then blurted out, "But you don't have the means to fulfil this contract!". My dad's solicitor, Mr. Shakespeare, then spoke for the first time, asking him how he knew that and that telling him that his statement was impugning the honesty of Mr. Kesseler. The seller's solicitor quickly told his client to shut up. **FAMILY STORY ALERT**. All of the previous is accurate, however, I was led to believe that there was a private agreement to stop Dad taking the seller to court and that settlement paid our bills for a few months thereafter.

The sale was completed, and E.H. Kesseler owned Banks & Davis Limited. But only for a few weeks. 49% of the shares were transferred to the friend who had put up the money. It would be another 7 years before Dad was able to buy him out and really become the sole shareholder in the company. By the way, he very quickly moved the company bank account and his own to the National Provincial Bank in Bennetts Hill.

Apart from holidays with my immediate family during these years, I also had a glorious holiday in Babbacombe, Devon, with Uncle Sid, Aunt Edie, and my cousin Michael. Two things I remember with great clarity was a visit to Kents Cavern in nearby Torquay. The guided tour concludes in what was then known as 'The Bear's Cavern' and, to show how deep underground we were, the guide told us to stand still, and he turned out the lights. The darkness was complete and Sid stage whispered, "Now find you own way out". The other memory was our visits to the Babbacombe Theatre to see their Summer Concert Party. This cast performed three different show each week with the usual mix of dancing, speciality acts, singers, and a comedian. The big difference with these 'end-of-the-pier' shows were that all the cast were expected to join in with the sketches and set pieces. Of course, it all revolved around the comedian and his ability to bring in the audience. The year we were there it was an unknown comic called Leslie Crowther. Babbacombe had a gift for discovering new funny men, the year before we were there the 'star' was Bruce Forsyth!

Another holiday, this time with Aunt Lil Hubbard and Uncle Tubby was to Cornwall, probably 1958. My asthma was a constant companion, but usually I could cope. Every now and then, however, I would get an attack which would effectively disable me. That happened on this holiday. Aunt Lil was so worried that she took me to a local GP. He examined me and then said that he had recently had some samples of a new treatment called Rybarvin. Would I like to try it? Since there had never been an offer of any treatment before, the answer was clearly yes. Rybarvin was a clear liquid (atropine contained in stramonium) which had to converted to a mist and inhaled. This was accomplished with a nebulizer, a glass body with a face mask on top and a rubber bulb on the bottom to create the mist. The doctor showed me how to do it, and, for the first time in my life, I felt an almost immediate relief. Rybarvin continued to be my saviour for many years to come until it was replaced by more modern inhalers.

Back at Camp Hill my unauthorised absences and failure to do set work had other consequences. Teachers could give you detention. Detention meant that you had to stay over in school for an extra hour. Detention evenings were Wednesday to Friday and all the miscreants would be gathered in one classroom under the supervision of a bored teacher and given more boring work to do. The normal detention was for an hour, but if a teacher was suitably annoyed, he could give you two hours. These would be served on consecutive nights. Each morning, at Assembly, the Head would solemnly read out the list of those in detention that evening, a public shaming. One Friday, the Head, a kindly old gentleman maned Tom Rogers, read my name and stopped. He turned the page of the detention book back a page, and then another. He then spoke the dread words, "Kesseler, come see me and me at the end of Assembly".

Nervously, I climbed the steps to the stage and approached the huge carved wooden Headmaster's chair. Mr Rogers had now moved on to reading the detentions for next week. "Kesseler,", he said, "you appear to have four hours of detention in a row. Can you explain why?". My plea that I was unlucky was not well received. "Your bad luck continues; I am giving you a further two hours!"

The truth is that I was out of place in a school which prided itself on intellectual ability and examination results. I had fluked the entrance examination and what I thought was good luck at age 11, was obviously the opposite with hindsight. There was no choice, however, so I ploughed on towards GCE's. I was 14 when I took them and I obtained 'O' level passes in English Language, Mathematics, General Science and, surprisingly, French. I had come close in Geography; the pass mark was 45% and I got 40%. I left Camp Hill happily that June, adding my hated school cap to the bonfire on the edge of the playground and promising never to go back.

My father had plans for my future employment. I was nearly 15 and had to plan for the life of a man.

CHAPTER 7 - WORLD OF WORK AND THE SIXTIES

My father would have loved me to be an engineer but realised when he tried to train me in the workshop when I was 13 that I was a lost cause! So, he decided that a good profession for someone with GCE mathematics would be accountancy.

He organised a place for me as an audit clerk with a company called Whitehill Marsh Jackson in Waterloo Street close to the council house in the city centre. The senior partner was a dour Scotsman from Edinburgh called Douglas J Moir. He wasn't keen on the arrangement because, prior to my employment, audit clerks had to pay their employer for the privilege of being trained! However, my small salary did give me a first taste of independence.

If I was to become a qualified chartered accountant, I would have to take a series of examinations. There was an exemption from the preliminary examination if you had 5 GCE 'O' levels. I had four! I had got close in geography and so I decided to take six months of study at Garretts Green Technical College and retake the examination. I failed again with 35% which was 5% less than I got in the original examination.

The job itself was less than satisfactory although I did enjoy going out on audits. One highlight was Benton and Stone limited in Aston Brook Street. I was sent to do a check in the comptometer department, a room filled with about 30 female comptometer operators. having just turned 16, I was a shy young man, and this was a baptism of fire. Walking into that room I was wolf whistled at and had my bum patted by one particularly forward young woman. Sexual harassment was rampant in 1960! However, I got through it and when I returned for the next audit in six months' time I was prepared to give as good as I got. I have to say that, looking back, I think I enjoyed it, but it would never happen today.

Having an income, albeit small, meant that I could improve my social life and it was at this time that I got my first real girlfriend. I had had friends who were girls before and I had gone out on "dates", but no real long-standing relationship. My friend, Dave Taylor, had by this time met the love of his life, Rosemary. She lived in Washwood Heath and had a friend called Glenys who lived quite close. We were introduced and started going out together. The cinema was a favourite, the Beaufort was within walking distance of her house, and we saw many films there. Dave and I would often meet at the bus stop on our way home and sometimes we would "double date".

Our relationship lasted about a year until she gave me the elbow. She worked at an insurance company and, apparently, there was a married man who was much more interesting and exciting than me.

During this time my job at Whitehill Marsh Jackson was going nowhere. With only four "O" levels if I was to progress, I would have to take the preliminary examination, and I had no intention of doing that. Mr Moir was very understanding but suggested that it was time for me to go. I obtained another post with a smaller accountancy practice, Goodkin & Co, whose offices were in a rather dilapidated building in Corporation Street opposite the lawcourts. The firm was run by two Jewish brothers, David and Simon, and I was the first non-Jew to be employed. It was an eye-opening experience.

On my first day I was introduced to the two other audit clerks and given some books to check. Any 11 AM coffee and biscuits were brought in and one of my colleagues put his hat on. "I wonder where he's going?", I thought. He went nowhere, drank his coffee, ate his biscuits, took his hat off and started work again! He was Eli Rabinovich, the son of the then chief rabbi of Birmingham, and, of course, had to cover his head when eating.

The full complement of staff at Goodkin & Co were the three audit clerks, the two principals and the two ladies who ran the front office. They were Sonya and Marsha. The former was a homely and lovely lady who looked after me well and the latter was just drop dead gorgeous. Unfortunately, way out of my league!

I enjoyed working at Goodkin & Co. and being in a mainly Jewish organisation learnt a lot about Judaism and, incidentally about my faith. David Goodkin and his brother, Simon, were prominent members of the Birmingham Jewish community and I was privileged to meet many of those who came to see them at the offices.

The work was much more varied than my previous job with many more small clients. One of those was a newsagent on Hurst Street, in many ways a very typical shop selling papers, magazines, tobacco products and confectionery. It wasn't until my second year in the job that I discovered they had a thriving trade in pornography from the back room!

The offices in Corporation Street were, frankly, a dump and the company soon moved to much more modern offices on New Street, next door to the Woolworth store. Here it was decided that the front office needed an office junior and a young woman called Kay was appointed. Like me, she was a Gentile, and that gave us reason to bond. Very soon she became my girlfriend. Kay was kind, considerate, and, for some reason, besotted with me. The only problem with the relationship was that she lived way across city in Great Barr.

However, my real problem relationship was with Mom. I was a stroppy teenager and, I think, she didn't really know how to cope with that, and we clashed constantly. It finally came to a head in 1961. Mom, dad, and the children had gone away on holiday leaving me alone in the house. On the Friday evening, before they were due back on the Saturday morning, I tidied the house as best as I was able. Then, late at night, I made myself a supper of beans on toast, ate it and went to bed. Saturday, I arose late, as usual, and the family were home. The first thing that happened was that mom berated me for not washing up after my supper. No recognition of the work that I had done, only a complaint for what I had not done. I know that this was only a small thing but for me it was the final straw. My memory is that I made no response, walked down the hall, packed a bag, and walked out of the front door.

I took the bus to Nans house and told what I had done. She made me get in touch with dad and let him know what had happened and put me up for the night. The next day, having spoken to dad, I moved in at 4 Selma Grove with aunt Lil and uncle Tubby and my cousin Sheila. These were happy times with Lil looking after me very well. Dad was really concerned about my leaving home but, once he was convinced that this is what I wanted to do and I was not coming back, he supported me. We started going out together on a regular basis, sometimes going bowling, sometimes dog racing. Those shared times were very important to me.

1961 was a hugely important time in my life because, as well as leaving home, I was about to meet someone who would change my life for ever and for better. Dave Taylor let me know that our best friend, Dave Johns, had got himself a girlfriend and it was time we met her. We met, as I remember, outside the Birmingham Hippodrome and I remember this slim, beautiful, dark-haired girl and wondering what she saw in Dave! Mean thoughts for a friend, I acknowledge, but she seemed so classy, and I was smitten. But she was my friend's girl, and I did nothing to let her know I cared.

Over that year Lynn, Dave, Kay, and I often went out together and enjoyed each other's company. Usually, at the end of the evening Kay and Dave would make their own way home while Lynn and I would travel on the bus together because we lived on the same side of town now that I was living in Yardley Wood and she lived in Sparkhill. On these journeys we got to know each other better but I still kept my feelings secret.

Christmas was when it was all to change. The first change was in re-establishing contact with Mom and the family. I had not gone back to Horseshoes Lane since leaving, except for going back to collect the rest of my things. However, in the week before Christmas, I went back to deliver Christmas presents for the family. They had, by this time, moved house. Not far, in fact just next door. 64 Horseshoes

Lane was a two-storey brick-built house next door to the bungalow at 66 where I had lived with the family. It had been built by a builder for himself and his family and it was a lovely property. When it came on the market dad decided to buy it for himself and sell the bungalow. My reception was friendly, and I was happy to see them all again.

On Christmas Eve, Dave Johns, Lynn, Kay, and I met at Dave's house. It was a strange evening with a muted atmosphere. As we left, Kay went home, via the number 60 bus into the city while Lynn and I transferred to the number 11 to go back to Yardley Wood and Sparkhill. During the journey Lynn explained why the atmosphere had changed that evening. She had told Dave that their relationship was over. If I said that I had mixed emotions, I would be lying. While I was sad for David, I was hopeful that this might give me an opportunity.

As it happened, I had already arranged to meet Lynn on Christmas morning to go with her to church. There being no buses on Christmas day, I walked from Lil's house to Philip Sidney Road where Lynn lived with her family at number 45. We walked down to Sparkhill Congregational Church on Stratford Road where she normally worshipped. On the walk back to her house I plucked up my courage and asked if she would come out with me. She said yes! There being no buses back, I borrowed Lynn's sister Marian's bike to ride back for my Christmas lunch, full of happiness.

In the evening Kay and I were due to go to a Christmas Party at my cousins Sheila Kesseler's house in Whitehouse Common Lane, Sutton Coldfield. I had no access to a phone and so, as arranged, we arrived separately. Unfeelingly I told her that evening that we were no longer a couple. She was, understandably, very upset and I called for her father to come and pick her up. Looking back, I can't understand how I could be so callous.

Of course, Kay and I would soon see each other again, at work. This did not make for a good working relationship but, I was soon to be going on my first date with Lynn. Memory tells me that it was to the cinema to watch 'In search of the Castaways' starring Hayley Mills and Maurice Chevalier. One of our next dates was to a party hosted by Sheila Taylor, a Camp Hill school friend of Lynn. She had been invited while she was still going out with Dave, and he still attended on his own! Very embarrassing, but I was equally stressed by meeting again many ex-Camp Hillians, that I had had mixed relationships with while at school. Specifically, Martin Briggs, a very clever individual who was also a competent guitarist and singer, and Baz Saywood who was a rugby player who always looked down on my lack of sporting ability. I didn't want to let Lynn down, so I played to my one strength, making people laugh. I got away with it; I think. One couple who were there who were to become great friends were Linda Paice and her husband to be, Graham Beck.

Quite soon Lynn began to meet my family. One of the first visit was to Uncle George and Aunt Flo. Flo was, at best, acerbic, and her first comment on looking Lynn up and down was, "Damn sight better than the last one!", Lynn didn't know how to take that. Our first visit to see mom and dad was, to say the least, interesting. By this time, they had moved into 64 Horseshoes Lane. The reception was welcoming, and all seemed well. Lynn reported later that her reception from Barbara and Jon was a little less than welcoming. Jon head-butted her and Barbara gave her a Chinese burn!

Our relationship continued to grow, and we were going out regularly. Lynn's mom wasn't that keen on me compared to Dave. He was polite, handsome, considerate to her and Norman. I was none of those things and was liable to meet Lynn after work and take her out there and then, with no means of telling her parents. They, of course, had no telephone at that time. I can only imagine how much I made them worry, but these were exciting times as we got to know each other better.

As our relationship grew others around us changed. The year before Dave Taylor and told me that his girlfriend Rose was pregnant. They got married, at Birmingham Registry Office, with me as best man. No reception, we just went back to Rose's house in Washwood Heath for sandwiches and a drink. There was no opportunity for a 'best man's speech' on that day, but I was honoured to be able to make it fifty years later as Dave and Rose celebrated their Golden Wedding. Dave took his new responsibilities very seriously. He was already working at Midland Counties Dairies where he was training to be an accountant. The money earned was not enough to keep him, his wife, and his soon-to-be born son. So, he took on a weekend ice cream round and started to do outside work as a bookkeeper for individuals and small companies. His workload was incredible, it meant that we saw less of him as a friend, but he was determined to make a life, and a good one, for his family.

For me it had always been obvious that accountancy was not going to be my lifelong profession and in 1963 that also became obvious to my father. The Ato Mop business which had begun some years ago was now a major part of Banks and Davis turnover. It was decided that now was the time to bring me into the family business. I was put in charge of the Mop department, looking after stock control, orders in and dispatched, and manufacturing. To be honest, although I was nominally in charge of the Department it mostly ran itself from the manufacturing point of view. The staff there, which included my godmother, Vera Price, knew exactly what they were doing and as long as I managed to tell them what orders to make and made sure that the stock of parts were there with which to make them, everything ran smoothly.

I got on well with the rest of the staff, but it was obvious that I was only there because my surname was Kesseler. I had no qualifications and few skills to offer the business. I suppose that my major achievement in the two years I spent there was learning to drive! I had some professional lessons, but I benefited enormously from many hours of practice in a minivan belonging to the company. My "qualified driver" during these times was George Roper. George was an uncle of Maisie, my stepmom, and had joined the family business after his mother, Ada Roper, had died and the shop that they had run together on Deritend High Street had closed. His main job was shearing metal in the guillotine shop, which he always pronounced as 'gull on tyne'. He did have a full driving licence, but he had not driven for very many years. This did not matter because all he had to do was sit next to me while I drove. I eventually passed my test, at the second attempt, and I was now a driver.

I never really felt comfortable at Banks and Davis and so I began looking for another opportunity which might take me in a different direction. I answered an advert for a trainee salesman's position with an international company called Lamson Paragon. Computers were just beginning to take off in the United Kingdom and Lamson Paragon had an exclusive range of pre-printed and custom printed computer stationery. They were looking to expand their sales force and I joined with 25 other young men starting with a six-week training course, residential in London.

Those six weeks were immensely enjoyable. We were all put in "digs" in Ilford. Mine were comfortable with a decent breakfast provided in the morning. We then took the train to Stratford East where the offices were situated and where we would have a day's training. Lunch was provided at the training school, and we were given an allowance for dinner in the evening. We were also being paid our full salary! This meant that you had 26 young men at loose in London with money in our pockets. We had a blast.

The training was exceptional, product training of course, but also lots of training on the theory and practice of salesmanship, something that the Americans took much more seriously than did we Brits at the time.

The social life, however, was the best part. Several of us were thrown off a tube train for doing the conga along the length, opening the interconnecting doors as we did which, of course, was completely illegal. The transport police were waiting at the station! Banks and Davis had allowed me to keep the old minivan "462UDH" and I had driven it down to London. One of the guys on the course that I got friendly with was an ex-Hong Kong policeman who had retired from the force because he could no longer stomach the corruption in the province. He was, he told me, "Through with helping people". One evening I had taken the van and him into town. As we were leaving and driving through Leicester Square, in pouring rain, a motorcyclist in front of us was involved in a nasty accident. Even before I could pull up at the curb my colleague was out of the car and running to help. I parked up him help direct traffic around the accident until the police arrived while he looked after the injured motorcyclist who, of course, was not wearing a crash helmet. He took off his expensive suit jacket folded it and put it under the patient's head. He put him into the recovery position and waited for the ambulance. When the authorities did arrive and took over, we went back to the minivan, both wet but with his suit ruined. I asked him why, considering he said that his days of helping people were behind him, he had rushed to help. "Training took over, I guess", he said. "I was helping him before I even started thinking about it."

At the end of the course the two main tutors took us trainees out for a meal. It was a disaster. The food was bad, the restaurant and bills worse. They felt so bad that instead of sending us home they took us onto a nightclub in Soho. It was a typical bustling place with gaming tables at one end and a bar at the other. We had been there for about half an hour when two large men walked in and walked up to the bar. It was as if somebody had turned down the volume as people stopped talking and started looking at these two heavyset men. They approach the barman, said something, he laughed and then they laughed. The relief of the tension in the room was obvious and slowly the volume came back. The Kray brothers were obviously not there to cause trouble, at least not on that night.

After we left that club and our tutors had gone home some of us stayed on partying into the night in Soho. About 12 of us went into a strip club. It was seedy and the "entertainment" was very poor. So bad, in fact, that one of our party joined the stripper on stage and did a much better job! This, to say the least, annoyed the club bouncers who chased us out of the club and down the streets. We split up to avoid them and eventually most of us met up at the station.

The next day was our last day at the training school but when we arrived only one of the two tutors was there. The other had gone to bailout the guy who had got on stage with the stripper the previous evening. Our last day was probably not the best!

I was appointed to a territory back in Birmingham and another young man on the course, Tony Dalziel, was given the other Birmingham territory. It seemed a good idea, since neither of us had a place to live in Birmingham at the time, to get a flat together. We found a bedsit in Norman Road, Northfield. It was basically a ground floor large room with two single beds and a kitchen/diner in a lean to at the back. Bathroom and toilet were shared with the other residents. It took some time but eventually we both got our company cars, green Morris Minors,

Tony was a decent flatmate, but he did attract the girls. I, of course, was going steady with Lynn, and he had a stream of visitors to our hovel. These he charmed by playing his guitar, singing gentle love songs to them while I would have to make myself absent. Although we both tried hard the job didn't work out for either of us. The problem was that we were selling computer stationery in a manufacturing city that hadn't yet caught up with computers! Tony eventually decided to leave (I believe he trained to be a Catholic priest!). I could not afford the Norman Road bedsit on my own and so began a tour of ratty lodgings across the city.

By early 1966 Lynn and I had been going out together for over three years and it just seemed to be accepted that some time we would get married. I don't remember proposing, but I do remember spending what seemed to be a lot of money on a beautiful solitaire diamond engagement ring. Lynn was completely accepted by my family by this time and my Nan was really taken with her. After trying a few different and short-term jobs after Lamson Paragon it was decided that I really should settle down into a stable position, preferably with a pension. I was interviewed by and got a job with The Treasurers Department at Birmingham City Council. It was, overall, pretty boring. Local government at that time was grossly overstaffed and those of us in the "books" department had less work to do than most others! We pushed two desks together, made a 'net' with books in the middle, and spent a good part of our day playing table tennis!

I think it is fair to mention at this point that I was continuing to be an unreliable partner to Lynn. Though we got on very well and we had a great deal of fun together on our own and with a growing circle of friends, Lynn got increasingly frustrated by my attitude to life and responsibility. I was also gambling at this time. The rules of the Gooden household at 45 Philip Sidney Rd meant that I had to have left the house by 11 PM. On many evenings, instead of going home, I would take the bus into the city and spend a few hours in one of the casinos. Needless to say, only the casinos ever win in the long term, which made my meagre finances even worse.

Lynn and I were originally planning to marry in late 1966 but my behaviour finally led to a flareup during which she returned the ring to me. I immediately pawned it and used the money to pay for a holiday at Butlins! This, in retrospect, seems callous, but the truth is that I was always trying to show that I was in charge and that nothing else intruded on me. It was, of course, a shell behind which I hid and, in the long-term was unsupportable.

By this time, I was living again with Aunt Lily Hubbard in Selma Grove, Yardley Wood. I had moved back here after the engagement so that I could save some money before the wedding. Big Lil was, as always, hugely supportive, as were the rest of the family. Lynn went round to see Nan to return her engagement present. Nan was having none of it, "you'll get back together again soon", she said.

She was right. I can't remember now how long Lynn and I were apart, but we soon renewed the relationship and started planning for a wedding a year later than we had originally expected. I made the effort to stay in the boring job at the council as we planned.

The date was set for September 23, 1967. My big regret about our having to change the date because of my behaviour was that Nan died in early 1967 and missed the wedding.

It seemed that much of 1967 was spent in planning. We had to find somewhere to live, and dad was kind enough to stump up the deposit on a house. We searched around for something that we both liked and could afford and found a small, modern, terraced house at the bottom of a cul-de-sac. This was 65 Westhouse Grove, off the Brandwood Road in Kings Heath. We didn't know it then, but it was to be our home for 21 years. Finding a mortgage was difficult. Lynn had a decent salary with the health service but mine was not enough, on its own, to secure the finance on a house. We needed to find a building society that would take Lynn's salary into account. Dad eventually found the Rowley Regis Building Society, in the Black Country, who would do that. We had found a house, and we had the means to buy it.

Planning for the service and reception also gave us some interesting challenges. Our church, Sparkhill Congregational Church, was without a permanent minister at this time and so we asked a friend who was a member of the church and had been a huge influence on my growth in faith over the last few years. His name was the Rev Henry Wightman who had spent a great deal of his life as a missionary in India and was, by this time a teacher. We found out later that he had never conducted a wedding before!

The problem of best man was also tricky. Since early in our relationship Lynn and I had always promised Dave Johns that he would be our best man if we ever got married. The problem was that over the last couple of years Dave had been suffering from serious mental illness. We now realise that he was bipolar, and he would veer from deep depression way he couldn't get out of bed to periods of manic behaviour where he would ring the AA for a chat at two in the morning because nobody else was available. It would certainly be a risk to give him the responsibility of being best man, but we felt, rightly, that this was our obligation. To give ourselves some wriggle room we asked Dave Taylor to be "second best man". His job, on the day, to look after Dave Johns and make sure that he was okay and on message.

The tradition in 1967 was that the costs of a wedding fell on the parents of the bride. Of course, my family had more available finance than Peggy and Norman, but tradition and obligation was followed, and they had to stump up most of the cost. They did, however, allow my dad to pay for an evening reception to follow the official "wedding breakfast".

Lynn was as practical as ever with her arrangements. She decided that since she would only ever wear a wedding dress once there was no point at all in buying one, so she hired one for the day. I and my ushers and best men were all decked out in hired dress suits. I arrived at the church early and, as the minutes ticked by, became more and more convinced that Lynn would see sense and not turn up! I busied myself by welcoming people to the church. The church magazine later reported, "Friends who were in good time for the Marriage Service of Blair and Lynn had the pleasure of being welcomed by the bridegroom. What a grand idea, but who but Blair would think of it, let alone carry it out and feel up to it. A beautiful service conducted by the Rev HS Wightman, surely God's spirit was at work on this happy day." Of course, the truth was that I was too nervous to sit down.

Lynn arrived, fashionably late, and Henry Wightman began the service. He dived straight in with "dearly beloved, we are gathered here together today....". Having done the formal business of marrying us he then opened the expensive, silver print, order of service and realise that he had completely missed out the first hymn. He bravely carried on, but "The Lord's my Shepherd" was never sung and has, therefore, been reserved for my funeral!

The reception took place at the Fox Hollies Community Hall and went well. Dave Taylor kept a close eye on our best man who had been warned that if his speech went on too long Dave Taylor would tell him to sit down. In fact, the speech was pretty good, but he did not have a finish. He began to ramble, and Dave Taylor stood up. Dave Johns saw him rise and immediately picked up his glass and said, "The Bridesmaids" and sat down. This reception was mainly family because we both have large extended families but, in the evening, we were able to invite friends to join us. Dad had booked a band, but they were frightful and much too loud, so he pulled out plugs on their amplification system and sent them home. Some of my relatives walked down the road to Vera Price's house coming back with a record player that gave us the music for the rest of the evening.

We had a cunning plan to escape at the end. During a dance we would unobtrusively dance out of the hall and into a waiting taxi before people noticed. That failed! Some of our friends noticed the taxi arrive and ambushed us and it with confetti. That confetti got everywhere, and I do mean everywhere. The taxi took us to The Midland Hotel in New Street. We apologised profusely to the taxi driver who would have had to spend a lot of time clearing out the confetti, and then we checked into our room for the night. It was an old-fashioned and very cold room which no amount of passion could warm up. It could only get better.

And it did get better. The next morning, we caught a train down to London for our honeymoon in the Strand Palace Hotel. Five days in London went by so fast, probably because we did so many things. Two theatre visits, to see Joe Brown and Anna Neagle in "Charlie Girl" and "Midsummer Night's Dream" with Cleo Laine as Titania and Bernard Bresslaw as Bottom. We also went to the cinema to see Sean Connery as James Bond in "You Only Live Twice". Of course, we did all the typical London tourist things.

Returning home meant moving into our new house at 65 Westhouse Grove together. Unfortunately, we were unable to complete the purchase of the property before our wedding day. This meant we had to leave Lynn's parents and cousin Brian to move in our furniture and get the house ready for occupation. Brian, of course, used the opportunity to decorate the outside of the house so that none of our new neighbours could be unaware that the newlyweds were moving in!

Thus began 21 years in this house. 21 years of many changes, many ups and downs and memorable moments. The house was at the bottom of a cul-de-sac which finished before you got to our house. From where the road ended there was a path with five terraced houses on either side. We were the last but one house on the right-hand side. It was compact with one through lounge and a kitchen on the ground floor, two decent size bedrooms and a small bedroom with a bathroom upstairs. Being fairly recently built it was modern and needed very little doing to it which didn't stop my new father-in-law tinkering with the electrics and fittings. A small front garden, mainly lawn, reached out to the central path and, at the back, there was a paved patio and a garden which rose steeply to the back fence. Beyond the fence there was an open space which, we had been told, was zoned for education, maybe an infant School.

For me this was an opportunity to settle down after many years moving from place to place and, for Lynn, an opportunity to build a home. We didn't have much money, not even enough for a television set at the start, but we loved that little house. A couple of streets away lived Lynn's cousin Brian and his wife Jean. Brian and Lynn had always been close and over the years that we were "courting" we had been to many parties together and had even been on holiday to London together.

Our first Saturday in our new house also coincided with the opening of BBC radio one, two, three and four. I remember very clearly waking early to turn the bedside radio to 247 m to hear Tony Blackburn say the opening words of the first pop radio station legally broadcasting in the UK. "And, good morning, everyone. Welcome to the exciting new sound of Radio 1". He then played "Flowers in the Rain" by The Move as his first record. The music of the 60s was very important to us sharply dividing "our music" from the music of our parents. Our generation were finding their feet and finding their place in a world which was scary. The Cuban missile crisis of October 1962 had brought the world very close to a nuclear confrontation between the Soviet Union and, specifically, the United States of America. The ongoing war in Vietnam, which many of our generation opposed both here and, in the USA, was another of those West versus communism adventures. Many people of our generation lived in genuine fear of a nuclear war and, for some, living for the future was not an option, the present was all that we had.

Once I had started going out with Lynn, after that first Christmas visit in 1962, I started to be a regular at Sparkhill Congregational Church. I was intrigued by the vast differences between this church and the Anglican churches where I had worshipped before. Firstly, it was completely independent, there was no hierarchy, deacons were elected by the congregation to represent them, and the Minister was called by the congregation. In fact, when I first started to attend the church was intent on getting rid of the current minister which they did! I had always been a democrat and so was keen to become part of this organisation.

I began worshipping there regularly and eventually was received into membership. This gave me the right to speak and vote at church meetings which was the government of the church. The other thing that impressed me was how welcoming people were. Thinking back to that first Christmas morning, I remember clearly being greeted by a very old man who came forward specially to shake my hand and welcome me into the church. I could never remember that happening to me before in any other church that I had visited. I discovered later that his name was "Pop" Ecclestone. He was the first of many people to make me feel a part of that congregation. There were many others including an old school colleague, Alan Perkins, who worshipped there with his parents.

Now that Lynn and I were a "couple", I started attending the church regularly with her. The difference between the Anglican services that I was used to was the lack of a liturgy and the more freewheeling attitude to worship in general. I found it very refreshing and began to become more involved in the life of the church.

There were a number of influential people within the congregation but none more so than the Wightman family. Carol was the church treasurer, and her husband Henry was a retired Congregational minister now working as a teacher. We began going to a Bible study group at their house which proved to be a huge part of my faith journey. I remember asking a question of Henry during one of these meetings. I cannot remember what the question was, but the answer has stayed with me for nigh on 60 years. His answer was simple, "I really don't know, that is something that has concerned me for some time." Not earthshattering, you would suppose, but for this young ex-Anglican whose betters had always expressed certainties, this showed to me that doubt could be valid. If this extremely experienced Christian could harbour doubts then, surely, it was reasonable for me. I have doubts right up to this day, but they have never overcome my faith since.

All marriages have their challenges, and my employment was to prove one of our first. City Treasurer's Department decided to move me to a branch office in St Mary's Row, Moseley. This was a small office, only two staff, that gave residents a convenient place to call in and pay their rates and other charges. The office was small, with a counter in the front where the money would be received, and a small office with a kitchen in the back. It was very convenient for me as all I had to do was walk to Alcester Lane's End and then catch the number 50 bus straight to Moseley village. All was good until the powers that be decided that the office was inefficient and too costly and that they were going to close it and, at the same time, end my employment. This led to the first of many financial crises in our early married life, most of them caused by me!

Lynn was working, as she had done since she left school, for the Blood Transfusion Service. She increased her income my doing occasional night duties when she would be on call from home and would be collected via driver if she needed to go in for any urgent work. In those early days we did not have a telephone and so it would be a knock on the door and then up and out. Lynn's job was our stability because over the next few years I lurched from one job to another. For a short time, I worked for Birmingham City Football Club in their Pools and Promotions division, raising funds for the club. I also worked in an employment agency, finding jobs for other people, and spent some time working in an electrical retailer shop. At one time, out of work and desperate, I even sold doorbells door-to-door. That may sound strange, but you can look at a door and immediately know if they have or have not got a doorbell. In other words, if all they have is a knocker you have a potential customer! We bought the bells wholesale and fitted them immediately. It would be some years before I had another settled job, but more about that later.

CHAPTER 8 - 1972 - 1984

I remember 1972 for two things, the birth of the United Reformed Church and re-joining the family business.

In 1972 the Congregationalists and the Presbyterians were in discussion to amalgamate and create a new church which would be called "The United Reformed Church". Congregational churches, being individually independent, would have to opt into the new church. There was much discussion before we at Sparkhill decided that we would go with the new denomination, and we became Sparkhill United Reformed Church. Part of our new constitution called for the election of elders. I was elected as one of the first batch in the new organisation.

My employment finally settled down in 1972 when I re-joined Banks and Davis, the family business. The business was doing well, especially the Mop division, where contracts had been negotiated with both the National Health Service and the Royal Navy. This gave us a solid base to build the business on and the company needed somebody else on the sales side.

The only full-time salesman employed by the company was Maurice Ryer, who was, officially, The London Area Sales Manager. There is no doubt about it, he was one of the best salesmen that I ever knew, a fact he was well aware of. Maurice would always want to be the centre of attention, and usually achieved that. He was sensible enough not to try and outshine his managing director, my father, Ted Kesseler. My dad always been a larger-than-life character, and this had helped him enormously to get to this point in his career.

I was taken on as Midland's area sales manager. This, however, was a complete misnomer because my territory covered everything from Cornwall to Glasgow. The only area that I didn't cover was the extended London area and I had no input to the negotiations with either of our big contracts. However, unlike Ryer, I had responsibility for selling the hollowware fittings part of our business. You always had to be on your guard when you were with Maurice, one-upmanship was a major part of his game. I first found this when asked to assist him at an exhibition aimed at hospitals and taking place at St Mary's Hospital, Paddington. We had a small stand, just inside the entrance, featuring the range of Ato-mops. Ryer helped me set up the stand but when one of his major London customers arrived, he went off with her leaving me on my own. I really think, looking back, that he hoped I would fail maybe thereby increasing his perceived status. I must admit that I was very nervous, but I certainly didn't show it when he came back and discovered two new orders in the order book!

Another story which illustrates the determination of Maurice Ryer to always be noticed occurred at a Cleaning Industry dinner. The invitation read "Evening Dress Will Be Worn". On the evening itself all the men were, of course, wearing dinner suits with black tie. In other words, all looking exactly alike. Except for Mr Ryer who was wearing evening dress, but Scottish evening dress! He was not Scottish, in fact his background was East End Jewish, but he certainly stood out!

Over the next two years I got to know the business well and developed my selling skills. I was travelling throughout the UK and the Republic of Ireland and enjoying it. The business was profitable and so I stayed at good hotels and ate at decent restaurants. I had a company car with all expenses paid and I liked driving. I also enjoyed the independence that being on the road gave me. In those days before mobile phones, I would attempt to telephone the office once a day from a public phone box. The office had no way of contacting me unless they left a message at the hotel I would be staying at. This gave me the freedom to be in charge of my own days, my own timing. If I got the calls done nobody cared how long it took. If all went well there were sometimes days when I could take a few hours to visit the local zoo or beauty spot. Over these years I got to see many of the lovely sights of our country.

The longer distance trips would be those to south-west of England, Scotland, and the Irish Republic. Devon and Cornwall I always kept for the winter months. There was no point in going during the summer where you would be fighting holiday traffic and paying top price for hotels. So those trips would be either in the autumn or in the spring. This gave me less crowded roads, cheaper hotels, and the opportunity to look at the resorts when fewer people were there.

My visits to Scotland were epic. I would leave Birmingham about 4 AM, take breakfast just after I crossed the border and hit my first appointment in Glasgow by 9:30 AM. I would do all my calls around that city during the day then drive to Edinburgh and my hotel for the night. Next morning, I would do my Edinburgh calls and then drive home. Looking back, I cannot imagine how I would put all those miles in during just two days. But then I was young. The Scottish business was entirely Mop-based, but Ireland was different.

One of our major holloware customers was situated in the Republic of Ireland, Irish Aluminium. That business was situated in a little town called Nenagh in County Tipperary. There were other customers that were based in and around Dublin and so my normal visit would follow this typical schedule. In the late afternoon I would drive to Liverpool where I would embark on the overnight ferry to Dun Laoghaire. Usually taking a small cabin I would get a little sleep on the journey across. Arriving in Ireland in the early morning I would take a leisurely breakfast and then make my calls in the capital. Finishing these, usually by mid-afternoon, I would make my way to my hotel. One of my favourites was the Green Isle Hotel situated a little way out of the city. Sometimes, however, I would stay in Dublin and enjoy a little of the nightlife. The next morning, I would drive cross-country to Nenagh, a drive that included crossing the Curragh. This was a great horseracing centre in Ireland and often I would see the horses being exercised.

Irish aluminium was by far the largest employer in the area and so held a great deal of sway over the town. When I started representing Banks and Davis there, after years of my father making the calls, the owner was Miss Barrett. Miss Barrett had been the housekeeper to the previous owner, and he had left her the business. I ought to say that this does not imply any "funny business", Miss Barrett, a lady of a certain age, would never have been involved in anything like that. She did not have any great business nous, but she could pick good people, and her management team run the business for her while she looked after the visitors.

This would sometimes involve lunch at one of the small restaurants in the town. I remember well, on my first visit, accompanying dad going with Miss Barrett and others to lunch at the pub. I was driving us in my dad's car and when we got to the town there was no parking spaces. No parking spaces, that is, except next to the petrol pumps on the Main Street. You saw this a lot in Ireland at the time, petrol pumps on the pavement and, of course, you didn't park in front of them because that would stop trade. But it was lunchtime, and they were closed, so Miss Barrett instructed me just to park in front of them. I did and we went in for lunch. About an hour later a flustered looking man came into the pub asking loudly who owned the Rover in front of his pumps. My father answered, "Ah, that'll be me". "And he's with me, Tony", said Miss Barrett. "Oh,", said the petrol station owner, "that's all right then, I wasn't expecting any trade anyway!".

These Irish visits were some of the highlights of my work with Banks and Davis and I still look back on them with a great deal of warmth.

1973 was a momentous year, the year we stopped being a couple and became a family. I had not been keen to have children, probably afraid of the responsibility, but that changed after our friends, Ken and Cheryl Plant, adopted their first daughter, Emma. We went to visit them, and I still remember the big, brown eyes of that adorable little girl. Her looks and the obvious joy of her parents changed my mind.

By the time we went on holiday to Scotland, we knew that Lynn was pregnant. We started that holiday with a week in Fort William, in the shadow of Ben Nevis. We were camping in our old ridge tent and the week started well. Then, it began to rain and, being Scotland, it didn't know when to stop. By the time we packed up to move on to

Skye the tent was sodden There is a photo where you can see the standing pools of water on the campsite. We drove to Skye and the weather changed, the sun came out and Portree looked beautiful. It was obvious that the tent was too wet to set up again so, with the aid of the local tourist office, we found a simple caravan on a farm, where we had an idyllic week. (photo with chickens)

Our other holiday that year was a short break to Dubrovnik, then a part of the communist state of Yugoslavia. We stayed at the Hotel Astarea in Cavtat, a short bus ride from the walled city of Dubrovnik. The old town was amazing, the main street being paved with marble, so it glowed at night and glistened by day. We hired a car for one day and drove away from the coast. The roads were narrow and in one place had a steep drop on one side. We had no ide where we were going but eventually arrived at a little village called Trebinje. I remember clearly a beautiful small mosque in the centre of the town. The next time I heard of the town was during the Serbian/Croation war of 1991, when it was shelled to destruction.

Dunstan was born on December 13th, 1973, in the Maternity Hospital on the Queen Elizabeth site. We had both gone to the parenting classes and so I thought I was prepared, but, of course, I wasn't. Lynn was late and so they called us in for her to be induced. The staff couldn't be kinder and more helpful. We were in a private room waiting for the process to move on. Lynn began to feel sick, so I went out in the corridors to find a nurse. When I did, she came quickly, but told me that, if it happened again, not to go looking, but to press the call button. An hour or so later, Lynn's nausea returned and so I pressed the call button. Imagine our surprise when a trolley came crashing through the doors, followed by a doctor and a team of medics. I had pressed the wrong button and summoned the Crash squad! After being told that there wasn't an emergency, they left quite amused, luckily for me.

Maybe that got Lynn on the move and Dunstan arrived later. I was able to attend the birth, something quite new in maternity care, and I held Lynn's hand and encouraged her through the pains. He was a large baby and slightly blue when he was born and was quickly put into what looked like an aquarium with an oxygen feed. While the staff looked after Lynn, I was told to look after my baby and turn the oxygen flow off when he turned pink. I was a dad, with all the responsibilities that that privilege brought with it.

The following year we took two holidays, although one was business related. In April we took a canal holiday on a tiny cruiser on the Shropshire Union Canal. With Dunstan only 5 months old, we travelled up as far as the Llangollen Canal. One event stands out in my memory. Lynn wasn't too keen on driving the boat, so when we came to locks or swing bridges, she would handle those while I drove through. Until the Llangollen, that is. The lift bridges on that canal were operated by jumping up, holding the rope and using your weight to open the bridge. Lynn was just not heavy enough! She hung there, dangling ineffectually. So, we had to swap roles. Lynn stayed on the boat, I opened the bridges, she pulled to the side, and I got back on the boat. All fine until, after one bridge, the boat was not by the bank, and Lynn was nowhere in sight. Obviously, the baby needed attention and she had gone below. I looked at the distance between the bank and the boat. I calculated that I could jump it. I jumped and landed safely on the side of the boat. Then promptly fell off! Hanging to a rope, I shouted, "Lynn, Lynn, I've fallen in!". She came up on deck, carrying Dunstan, and laughed so much she had to sit down. I lowered myself into the shallow canal and walked back to shore, wet, muddy and chastened. The rest of the holiday was fine.

Later in the year, our little family went off to County Tipperary, mixing business at Irish Aluminium, with a stay at the Inn in Dromineer, down by the lake. Looking back, I think we were very brave in taking a baby on the ferry and staying in hotels, but we knew no better and had a great time.

Maybe becoming a father made me start thinking more about the world that Dunstan would be growing up in and, hoping to do my little bit, I joined the Liberal Party in 1974. My interest in politics had started back in secondary school and I had developed an affinity for the Liberals who, under their charismatic leader, Jeremy Thorpe, were beginning to make waves in the political establishment.

My intentions were simple. I intended to join the party, pay my dues, and maybe deliver a few leaflets in the October general election. I joined my local party in Birmingham, Hall Green, which covered the council wards of Billesley, Brandwood and Hall Green itself. The local hierarchy seem to be pleased to have me, but they rapidly developed plans I hadn't seen coming. Though the results in the October election were not as good as we'd hoped, local aspirations were still high and by December of that year I found myself being interviewed to be the local government candidate in my home ward. This was the start to a 20 year "career" in local politics. You will find more about my political life in Chapter 10.

In 1975 Maurice Ryer finally left Banks and Davis after another dispute with my father. I took over his responsibilities for London and the South and we brought in another salesman to help out. Mike Mangham was a charismatic young man with an easy attitude, and I found it easy working alongside him. Having the responsibility for London meant staying down there occasionally which gave me the opportunity to indulge my love of theatre.

In 1976 the National Exhibition Centre opened, and Banks and Davis exhibited at the very first show. For many years we had stands at exhibitions at both Earls Court and Olympia, but the difference in facilities, access and cleanliness was immense. It is true to say that the standards set in Birmingham caused the other exhibition centres in the capital to up their game. We showed our mop range and launched a smaller, and cheaper, version which we called "The Kestrel". The byline was "It Swoops on Dirt!". I thought it would be a good idea to try and get some press publicity and so approached the representative of the comedian Arthur Askey. One of the attractions at the NEC was a fitted theatre and Arthur Askey was booked to perform there during this exhibition. We arrange that he would do a press call on our stand one afternoon after he had finished his show in the theatre.

For the readers who don't remember Arthur Askey he had become hugely famous during the Second World War with his radio programme "Bandwagon". His career continued and he moved from

UNRELIABLE MEMORIES

radio to TV, all the while continuing to perform on stage and in pantomime. He was, at this time, 76 years old. Although this is two years younger than I am as I write this, to me at this time he was an old man. I went to the green room by the theatre to collect him after show and it was an old man that I discovered. He was sat slumped in a chair looking absolutely worn out after his performance. So concerned was I that, after being introduced to him, I offered to delay the press call while he recovered. He was having on of that, "I'll be fine son", he said, hauling himself out of his chair and following me to the door that led back into the exhibition hall. As he stepped through that door into the areas where the public were, the transformation happened. This little old man suddenly was on the balls of his feet skipping along the pathways, joking with passers-by and generally looking 20 years younger than when I met him!

The press were there when we got back to our stand, and he immediately charmed them. Since he was a very short man, we had made him a very short mop. He loved it, worked the audience gathered around with immense skill and left me with memories and a photograph that I still have.

Our range of mops also took me to exhibitions away from Birmingham. Two venues stand out. The cleaning exhibition at Waverley, Edinburgh was the worst I have ever attended. In most exhibitions you get quiet times, when there are only a few visitors around. At Waverly the hall was so empty that we had a running card school with the stands around us! To be fair to them, the organisers were so upset that they gave us a free stand at another event in Glasgow later in the year. Back in Edinburgh, I was on my own for most of that week, but Dad came up for one night, bringing with him my young sister, Barbara. After visiting the disastrous exhibition, we all retired to the bar at the Castle Hotel. As befits a first-class Scottish Hotel, it boasted a huge range of single malt whisky. Whisky was my dad's favourite tipple, and he took great care in choosing one, I chose my favourite and, of course, dad and I had them neat. Barbara picked hers, I think because it had a pretty label, and asked the barman to put orange in it. His face was a picture, this young

Sassenach was asking him to defile Scotland's national beverage. I thought for a moment that he was going to vault the bar and educate her, but his professionalism took over and with a quiet, "Certainly, madam" he ruined a very good, very expensive whisky.

The best venue I went to in those years was the RAI exhibition hall in Amsterdam. By this time our agreement with Josef Blum and Leifheit had come to an end and we were free to export the Ato-Mop and set our eyes on Holland. We were relatively successful, and did two exhibitions there, two years apart. Staying in that great city was a pleasure and I did have some time to investigate the charms of Amsterdam and fall in love with Indonesian cooking.

Of course, setting up an exhibition in Europe in those pre-EEU times, was complicated. Your exhibits had to be certified, then crated up by authorised shippers, who would then deliver them to you in the RAI hall the day before the exhibition. At the end of the exhibition, the shippers would arrive, re-crate all the items and take them back to our factory in Birmingham.

We had a demonstration machine. It was a simple construction with an electric motor concealed in a hollow aluminium body, which moved a mop up and down on a wet paving slab. The idea was to show how resistant to wear the sponge was. It had a display that said, "The sponge on this Ato-mop has now travelled XX miles on rough concrete". We had used it for years on our exhibitions and was always a conversation starter.

On our second visit to Amsterdam, we had a young salesman, very enthusiastic and single. He really enjoyed what Amsterdam had to offer, in all the ways that you can imagine. When the time came to pack up on the last day, he was keen to disassemble the display machine and help install it in its crate. A couple of weeks later, when the equipment was delivered back to us, he was hanging round, quite agitatedly. When he volunteered to unpack for us, a job that would normally be done by one of the labourers, I became suspicious. I was right, he had packed the machine casing with Dutch pornography! He swore it was for his own use, but I had it burned anyway. Not from prudishness, you understand, but because there was no way I was going to collude in him making a profit on my time! To be fair, he stayed with us for some time and was a good salesman.

As all this happened, our family grew. Sadie Louise was born on October 28th, 1975. This time the birth was not delayed, in fact we arrived at the hospital just in time. By the time I had changed for the delivery room, she was well on the way. Our family was now complete, and our life was good. We were lucky too in having built in baby-sitters in Lynn's young sisters, Christine and Jill. We abused their kindness unmercifully, leaving them to look after our kids while we went out enjoying ourselves. My life was, by now, complicated with politics which took up much of my time, which I will describe in a separate chapter.

Back at work, my travels continued. Of course, not every overseas visit was pleasurable and one, in fact, bordered on terrifying. In 1982 we were contacted by Mr Felix Anagara who was intending to build a hollowware factory in his home village in southern Nigeria. He was looking for a company to supply him with handles. It looks as if it could be a very good contract to have and so we took advice about travelling to Nigeria and doing business in that country. In particular I spoke to someone who was experienced in dealing with Nigeria and he gave me a few notes. One of them was that, at that time, the whole Nigerian system ran on backhands and bribery. I didn't like that, but it was obvious that that was the only way that business would be done.

Having made my preparations, I flew from London to Lagos international airport. Part of my preparation, that I needed to register all the currency I was carrying because, except for the local currency, naira, I would have to account for any spending done in the country before I could leave. Knowing that, I went straight to the currency desk as soon as I had cleared customs and then went to make my way out of the airport, only to be stopped by armed guard who pushed me in the chest with the butt of his weapon and told me I had to go to currency. I explained that I had, and he let me through. My first experience with a very different culture.

I then took a taxi to the Lagos internal airport where I was due to catch my connection to Enugu, in the south of the country. My tickets were pre-bought but, of course, you do not get on a plane without a boarding card. I got in the queue. I watched those in front of me put their ticket in front of the officer alongside a small "gratuity" in the local currency. This, I had been told about and was expecting. When I reach the front of the queue, I did the same, and receive my boarding card.

I left the queue to try and get towards the boarding gate because I had been told that it wasn't unusual for them to "sell" more boarding cards than there were seats on the plane! I had just got comfortable when I felt an arm on my shoulder. The arm was attached to a uniformed police officer. I was, then and there, arrested for bribing a customs officer. Bundled into a car, I was driven to the local police station, adjacent to the airport. Needless to say, I was terrified. A long way from home and frightened about what might happen next. What happened next was that the police made it quite clear that all charges will be dropped in exchange for a little money. However, this bribe would have to be paid in either sterling or American dollars. There was no choice, I paid. Then with many smiles I was put back into the police car and driven back to the airport. My plane was already sitting on the tarmac with a long queue snaking back from the steps. The police car drove straight to the front of the queue and put me there. This, as you could imagine, did not make me popular with the people behind.

Having boarded, we took off in a modern jet airliner which appeared to be piloted by somebody who had done his training in a fighter plane. I still cannot believe how tightly that plane could bank as it left the airport. At this point I was hoping that my baggage was on board because I hadn't seen it since I arrived at the airport, but when we landed at the very small Enugu airport and ushered into "baggage reclaim" there was no conveyor belt, no carousel, just two very large gentlemen who would read out the name on a piece of luggage, shout the name out loudly to the gathered crowd, and then throw the baggage towards the person who'd indicated it was theirs!

The good news was that my baggage was there. I was supposed to be met at the airport by a representative of the company I was visiting, but there was no one there. No mobile phones of course and having waited some time I took a taxi to the hotel where I knew I had been booked, The Presidential Hotel.

When I checked in, I was told that there had been a breach in the main water main leading to the town and that water was restricted to the one jug that was in my room which I would have to use for all purposes. I then managed to contact the company and, from here on in, things got much better. They were distraught that they had not been there to meet me, but they were expecting me on the following day and Mr Anagara was actually in Lagos and expected to return later that evening. They quickly arranged that two directors would come and dine with me that evening before taking me to meet my host at his home.

When the company's representatives arrived, they were very helpful with the arrangements at the hotel, obtaining me more water and an electric fan, very important in what was oppressive heat. The three of us went into dinner in the dining room which was very impressive. The hotel was colonial, if slightly rundown, the waiters, wearing white shirts and red jackets looked very impressive. The menu was a leather bound with gold imprint. Unfortunately, when I opened it there was only one option for dinner, turkey legs! I ordered the turkey legs.

After the meal we drove to Mr Anagara's house, a beautiful place on the outskirts of town surrounded by high fences which were being patrolled by armed guards. My host, when I met him, could not have been nicer. Following the Biafran war, he had built up a business and a fortune in the motor trade and now wanted to bring jobs back to the village in which he was born. We drank champagne together and toasted the potential business before I went back to my hotel for an uncomfortable night under my mosquito net.

The next morning, I was collected, and we drove to the village where the factory was to be built. We began on a very typical motorway, but shortly turned off onto roads that lead through what I would describe as sparse jungle. I couldn't help but notice when we made one sharp turn that ahead of us was a burnt-out truck that had obviously run into a tree. Then, a little later, at another turning there was another smashed up truck. When I saw the third one, I asked my companions what was happening. They explained that truck drivers were paid, not by the hour, but by the delivery. Distances tend to be long in Nigeria and so they would chew a stimulant to keep them awake. Unfortunately, this sometimes led to the eyes being open but the brain receiving no information and, coming to a sharp turn, driving straight on!

We arrived in the village to a rapturous welcome. It was obvious that Mr Anagara was a local hero. I was introduced to the local team, shown where the factory would be built and then the little visiting group was treated to lunch. They actually killed a chicken for us! In the afternoon we returned to Enugu, and I left there the next day. Arriving back in Lagos the feeling that I was under scrutiny at all times would not go away and I only felt comfortable when the plane to London was actually in the air. It had been an instructive but unsettling visit. When I got back to Birmingham, I sent off our offer but, after all this effort, we did not get the business. I found out later that it had gone to Heinrich Baumgarten Gmbh in Germany.

With the children growing up, Lynn returned to work in 1982. She obtained a new post back at her old employers, The Blood Transfusion Service. She was to remain there until her retirement. The immediate effect of this lifestyle change was to improve our finances! I have never been good money management and the extra income made a big difference.

Over the years Banks and Davis had met various challenges and had continued to prosper. To cut costs dad had sold part of the premises to our next-door neighbours and concentrated at 44 to 47 River St. As my father got older, he wanted to relinquish some responsibilities so I, eventually, became Managing Director. He remained as Chairman and my sister Barbara joined the Board. This meant the board consisted of my father, Maisie, myself, Barbara and

Geoff Madeley, our company secretary and accountant.

Geoff was a lovely man, completely honest and a devout Christian. His accountancy advice was invaluable to the company and helped us negotiate some of the problems that we met along the way.

One of those was the problem of being overstaffed at a time when business was difficult to come by. The advice from Mr Madeley was that we would have to slim down and make many people redundant. We looked at the full staff list and decided on who would have to go. It is still by far the most difficult decision I have ever been part of. I had known some of these people for most of my life and I, as Managing Director, would have to inform them that they were no longer employed. I did take the decision to do this with each individual, face-to-face, because I thought then, and I think now, that that was the right thing to do.

We did it all within one day, calling in each individual to tell them the bad news and to inform them of their rights and what redundancy they were entitled to. The last to be brought in was Fred Taylor who had been in charge of the factory floor for as long as I could remember. He, obviously, knew of our plans about redundancy, but could not believe that he would have been one of those to be let go. He was related to the Lee family, but this decision would mean that he would not speak to me ever again. However, it did buy the company many more years.

My time with the company came to an end at the end of 1983. By this time my brothers Edward and Jonathan had joined the board and, although I had the title of Managing Director, the board often had plans which I did not completely agree with or would reject plans that I put forward. This was board democracy about which I could not, and would not complain, but it did make relations difficult. I made the difficult decision to leave and negotiated a redundancy package which would see me over for a little time while I set up my own business.

CHAPTER 9 - WORK LIFE 1984 - 1994

The idea of working for myself was one that I had been thinking about for some time. I had been interested in computers for years and I had taught myself to program in Basic even writing a costing program for Banks and Davis.

So I bought a portable Microsoft PC together with a good accounts package. and started to look for clients. I found a couple for whom I did bookkeeping and some stock control. I also wrote a number of bespoke programs for customers.

I wasn't making much money but just enough to get by when I got a call from Dad. He said that Baumgarten in Germany were looking for someone to represent them in the UK. He asked if I would go over and negotiate with them on behalf of Banks and Davis. We negotiated and agreed on a fee, and I flew off to Germany to meet Rolf Baumgarten and Dick Taselaar. The negotiations went well except for one thing which was rather embarrassing. The truth was they didn't want Banks and Davis to represent them, they wanted me and thought I still worked for Banks and Davis. You may remember my journey to Nigeria and the fact that I didn't get the business after travelling all that way. Dick Taselaar, who was the export director for Heinrich Baumgarten had followed me into Nigeria and it was him who obtained the business. Although, in my mind, I had failed at this trip, I obviously impressed my German competitor.

In all conscience, I could not accept the dealership on my own behalf, but negotiated an agreement that all business would be passed through Banks and Davis, but I would subcontract to them and effectively be the representative in the UK. On return to Birmingham, my father and I agreed my remuneration and also that

I would have use of an office in River Street so that calls about Baumgarten could be received on the Banks and Davis switchboard.

For the next two and half years I had the great pleasure of representing Baumgarten in the UK and going to Germany for the international trade fair at Frankfurt, where I would stay with the Baumgarten family in a little town called Neunkirchen, where their business was based. Staying with the Baumgarten family was luxurious. They had a large family house with a guest wing in which customers and their overseas representatives like me would be accommodated. Rolf also had an extensive wine cellar, and we would spend evenings drinking great wine and talking business.

Alongside my work for the German company, I was continuing with my other business based around computers. At this time, I had a couple of friends who were "proper" computer programmers, Mick Gibson and Trevor Carter. It was Trevor who came to me with an opportunity. He had done a little work for a company called Raydek Safety Products. They were having some trouble with their recently installed computer system, and he didn't have the time available to work on it. He introduced me to the company, and they gave me the job of getting it up and running. Very soon it became obvious that they had been terribly advised by their supplier, BT, and that the system was not up to the job that had been specified. I told the managing director, Derek Campbell, that this was the case and that was no point in paying me to waste time trying to make it work. He asked my advice on what they could do, and I said the only thing I could suggest was that they get BT to take the equipment out and refund them with the costs. Of course, it wouldn't be that easy, and so I was asked to write a comprehensive report on why the system was unsuitable for the specification. This was submitted to BT, and, after discussion, they agreed with my suggestions.

Derek Campbell, the MD, was very impressed with my work and call me in for a discussion. He was considering an expansion into the computer market and asked me for my advice. I suggested that one area where I saw a deficiency in the market was a complete package for small businesses, including a PC, preloaded with word processing, spreadsheet and accounting software and a printer. He liked this idea and asked me to write it up and do some research for which he would pay me. I did this and presented a business plan. The next move surprised me!

He told me that he was going to set up a subsidiary company, called Raydek Technology and would like me to join the organisation and run it. At the time, I was happy being a freelance and working for Baumgarten. So, I said no. Derek persisted, asking me what salary would convince me to join the organisation. I plucked a silly amount from the air, and he agreed! I was hoisted on my own petard. The salary was very generous, and I felt that with the investment that the MD was promising the business could be successful.

Having talked to Lynn, I decided to accept the offer, which meant that I would have to do relinquish my post with Baumgarten. That representation was passed on to the new MD of Banks and Davis.

In 1987 I began work at the Raydek premises on the Saltley Trading Estate. A new mezzanine floor was installed at one end of the building with part of it being sectioned off the storage and the other part made into an office for me, my PA and a young engineer. The hardware was bought in, the software sourced, and we were in business. However, very soon the initial promises began to evaporate. The advertising budget was cut to almost zero which meant that getting leads became very difficult. Some did come from the other businesses in the group, Raydek Nameplates and Raydek Safety Products. Cold calling was also tried.

Where business was obtained the customers were usually very happy, but there were not enough customers for us to be profitable. Without the investment promised the business plan was unsustainable and within a year it was decided to close the business down. To be fair, I expected this to lead to my being dismissed but Derek Campbell offered me a move to Raydek Safety Products Ltd. This was, basically, a mail order business supplying safety products and signs to businesses across the country. I became Number Two to the general manager of the company, a very efficient lady called

Heather Pimble. We got on straightaway. We had a team of seven young women who answered the phone enquiries, taking orders and arranging dispatches. Heather and I sourced the equipment and laid out the catalogue which was the basis of the business. Heather soon found that I had some experience in page layout and publishing and that became one of the mainstays of my job.

Although this wasn't the job that I had sought, it became one that I really enjoyed. Heather and I were a good team and got on well with the girls. We issued two catalogues a year and desktop publishing them was a real challenge to my skills and would often entail staying in the office until 10 PM at night to make sure that we hit print deadlines. For almost 5 years the job continued to be rewarding and enjoyable.

Our little house in Westhouse Grove was, as our children grew, was becoming too small and in 1987 we began to look to move. This proved to be more stressful than we had anticipated. We finally settled on a property and made an offer, which was accepted. However, someone offered more, and we were gazumped! Back on the search, we found a terraced house in Barn Lane, close to Kings Heath centre and with four rooms downstairs instead of the two at Westhouse Grove. Upstairs the same three bedrooms, but larger. We made an offer and, this time, no problems, we were in. We moved on December 6th, 1988. Moving is always traumatic, but this didn't go well. After the kids had gone to bed in their new rooms, Lynn sat on a packing case and burst into tears. "I don't want to live here!", she wailed. After many changes to 45 Barn Lane, we are still there, 35 years later!

Back at Raydek, our managing director, however, was, to say the least, erratic. Always full of ideas, most of them not viable, quick to anger but, when in a good mood, good fun to be with. Over the years I got to be quite close to him and his wife. He would ask me for my advice on business matters and would often take me on visits to his accountants because he thought that with my background, I might understand their jargon better than he.

Our part of the business continued to grow, and Heather and I felt secure in our position. Then things changed. Derek, the MD, became notable by his absence. Someone who had been always present became an occasional and invisible visitor. The factory unit had three entrances. One at the front for the factory employees, one in the centre which was the main entrance to reception and also used by the office employees and one at the rear of the building which led straight into the MDs office. We realise that Derek was coming in occasionally using his own private entrance and only communicating with his general manager. This, of course, started rumours. He was ill. He was terminally ill. He had been disfigured and wouldn't be seen. Of course, the only one who really knew was the general manager, Chris Harris, and he was saying nothing.

One day, standing at the coffee machine listening to the current gossip about our MD I heard one of my fellow employees remarking that Derek's fingernails had gone shiny, as if this were a result of some affliction. Suddenly, I believed I knew what was happening. Derek had always been somewhat effeminate, and I guessed that he had now taken the next step. I went to Chris Harris and asked him outright, was Derek transitioning into a woman. With a great deal of embarrassment, he refused to answer but the next day I was called in and told my guess was correct. Derek had become Diane and had moved out of the marital home and into a flat in Moseley. I was invited to go and meet her. This I did, with some trepidation, but I was greeted well, and she didn't look too bad as a woman.

This began quite a time of meeting a number of transsexuals, one of whom ran another safety business. Some were extremely glamorous, some were very ordinary, but I had no problems with any of them. Diane eventually plucked up the courage to come into the office and be seen by the other employees. I'm sure that you, dear reader, can imagine the different attitudes across the business but, in general, we got on with doing the work we were employed to do.

The pressure of working at Raydek was heavy and holidays were important breaks to re-charge the batteries. One of the best came in 1991. Lynn and I have been blessed with good friends throughout our lives, with some going back to schooldays. Three girls who were at Camp Hill Grammar School for Girls with Lynn were Cheryl Plant, Linda Beck and Christine Kenney. Not only were they friends but we had all married within the same 12 months in 1996/7 to Ken, Graham and John respectively. It seemed a good idea to plan a joint holiday to celebrate, albeit early, our Silver weddings!

Calling ourselves the Silver Eight, we planned a villa holiday in Portugal in a little village called Guia. We planned the holiday very carefully with many meetings that involved wine and food! I issued a press release to the local media about eight school friends still married to their respective partners after 25 years and the Birmingham Mail sent a photographer to record the event. The photo made the front page of the Mail on the day we left in September 1991.

Guia was notable because Cliff Richard had bought a villa there with an orange orchard which he was transforming into a vineyard. The local restaurant, rather grandly called the Palladium, was our diner of choice and, on our last night, we were invited to sign the visitors' book. There was Sir Cliff's signature, with an added inscription from a needy fan. It read 'This is probably the closest I will ever get to you, Cliff".

The holiday was a great success. The weather was great, the area beautiful and the company brilliant. It was so good that we reprised the idea more than once.

Heather and I continued to run the Safety Products business without a great deal of interference until Derek/Diane decided to employ a friend of his, Mr Preedy, as a consultant. He was embedded into an office and became a distraction to the working principles. Meanwhile, an offer to buy the business had come in from one of our major competitors. We had known about this in advance because they had made a tentative approach to Heather. Not knowing this Derek/Diane summoned both of us to the office. The offer was worth £2 million, and he asked if we thought he should accept. We pointed out that he was the sole shareholder and that that 2 million would set him up for the rest of his life and he would still have the remaining business to occupy himself. He was not convinced, he thought that if the opposition thought it was worth 2 million it was properly worth more and he turned down the offer.

A few months later, just after lunchtime, Heather and I were again summons to the managing director's office, this time to be told that we were being made redundant with immediate effect. We were given 45 minutes to clear our desks and leave. No explanations were given just those instructions and that we would be paid according to redundancy law. We were, of course, both shattered. There had been no indication that this was likely to happen or that management were dissatisfied with us in any way. Just to make a point we did not leave quietly but stood by the clocking out clock to shake hands and say goodbye to everyone in the factory.

Redundancy is never easy to take, it is always a slap in the face and makes you consider your value. I had spent seven years of my life at Raydek, and I had always given of my best. I remember the 14-hour days when we were putting a new catalogue together, which we did twice a year. I remember being Derek/Diane's confidant and the feeling that he felt I was important to the business. And suddenly, in 45 minutes, that was all gone.

Heather and I met and decided that we would try to launch our own safety products catalogue, and we did, but without the exposure of our previous employer had, it was doomed to failure.

As before, I went back to doing odd jobs for other people and was then approached by one of Raydek's suppliers, a fabricating business whose owner wanted me to come in and manage the company. It seemed too good an offer to refuse, especially since he was matching my previous salary, but it soon became apparent that there was a very shady side to the way that the business was run. Finances were unstable and the bookkeeping was being manipulated so that cash flow could continue. Much work was being done "off the books" and after the first two months I realise that my main job was to cover up the illegalities. I quit.

Unemployed again I began to cast my net to see what opportunities might come up, either short-term or long-term. I was soon to discover a "short-term" opportunity which was to change the rest of my working life.

My sudden lack of a job also meant a sudden lack of income and changes had to be made. By now the 'Silver Eight' had welcomed the addition of friends Graham and Rita Spicer. The ten of us had been planning a holiday in France, renting a small chateau some miles from Bordeaux. It was quickly obvious that we could not afford to go, and so we apologised to our friends for letting them down and asked them to plan the visit without us.

A few weeks before the due date, they told us that the holiday was now paid for and that we were going, like it or not. They would meet all the expenses and we, in return, would undertake the cooking duties at the chateaux! Overwhelmed by their generosity, we accepted. We travelled by ferry driving through the town of Arromanches, the site of 'Gold Beach' in the D-Day invasion. Whilst there we booked a small hotel for the last night of our holiday as we returned to the Normandy Ferryport.

The chateaux itself was magnificent, bedrooms on three floors, a games room, a dining room that was like a banqueting suite and a well-equipped kitchen for Lynn and me to cater for our friends. There was even a goat which acted as waste disposal, because it ate all the scraps! For financial reasons, Lynn and I were not able to go off on the excursions with the others, but we had a wonderful time at the Chateau du Planty in Saint Christine.

On our way back, when we arrived at Arromanches, they were preparing to celebrate the 50th anniversary of liberation. We English were so welcome, and the hotel (L'Ammonite) treated us like honoured guests.

This holiday reminds me still of the value of good friends and we are still grateful that, though we could not contribute financially, our friends still wanted us with them.

CHAPTER 10 - POLITICS LIBERALLY SPEAKING

I had always had liberal tendencies, but 1974 was when I finally announced my political allegiance publically. In February of that year a General Election was held, but with no clear majority. Harold Wilson tried to form a coalition, but failed and formed a minority government. The Liberal Party under the leadership of the charismatic Jeremy Thorpe more than doubled its number of seats in the House of Commons from 6 to 14. This surge in popularity made me decide it was time for me to stop being liberal and become a Liberal. Later that year I joined the party.

My first efforts were campaigning for the second General Election in that year, in October. With my additional help the number of Liberal members in the house went from 14 to 13 and Harold Wilson had a majority. My record of losing elections was off to a start. It was a great demonstration of the in-built unfairness of our electoral system with the Tories winning 257 seats with 35.8% of the vote while the Liberals got only 13 seats with 18.3%. This, of course, has been the same throughout my political life and still, in my opinion, is not just unfair, but has robbed the country of the service of many talented people from across the political spectrum.

Personally, I was thrown in the deep end. A candidate for the Brandwood ward of Birmingham was needed and, since I lived in the ward, I was put forward. This meant that I needed approval from the regional party to stand as a potential councillor and I was summoned to West Midlands Party Headquarters, which turned out to be a dingy set of offices in Essex Street. The Regional Party Organiser was a rather reserved gentleman called Roy Lewthwaite, but I was not important enough to be interviewed by him and the responsibility was passed to his young assistant, Mike Ward. (Mike eventually became a long-serving councillor, I never did!). I passed the test and began my campaign. The Hall Green Constituency Liberal Party was led by its chairman, Don Hale, and we fought a unified campaign across the three seats in the constituency, Brandwood, Billesley and Hall Green. History shows that we didn't win a seat! My personal result gave me 12.2% of the vote. Across the city we won just three seats in Aston, Newtown and Duddeston, where Bill Doyle won over 60% of the vote. Bill was an unapologetic working class liberal and had a great effect on my thinking.

I fought Brandwood a number of times thereafter, always with the same result. The electors rejected me on a regular basis. So, I began to focus my efforts at internal offices, eventually being elected as the Chair of the Birmingham Party.

My political 'career' lasted from 1974-1994. In that time, I played the roles of defeated local government candidate (regularly), Chair of the Birmingham Liberal Party, President of the West Midlands Liberal Party, First President of the West Midlands Liberal Democrats and, for many years, Chief Agent for the Liberals in Birmingham. I could fill much more than one chapter with my thoughts and experiences over those two decades but, rather than a list of what happened when, I have decided just to feature some of the highlights of those years and some of the characters that played a big part in my political life.

The first major event that I was involved in came in March 1977. Roy Jenkins, the Labour MP for Stechford, had been widely tipped to be the Chancellor in Jim Callaghan's government but was overlooked. Instead, he took up the invitation to be President of the European Commission. This meant a bye-election in Stechford, and the Liberal Party, having a surge in the polls at the time, decided to contest it. Our candidate was a local councillor, Graham Gopsill, a colourful character in Birmingham politics. With money from the national party, we rented a large house in the constituency for our headquarters. This was my first experience of national politics, and I was there every evening and through the weekends. At first there was optimism bolstered by visits from our leader, David Steel. After the first two weeks, however, there was an obvious swing to the Tories and our vote was being squeezed.

Although this dampened enthusiasm, it didn't stop the invasion of helpers from all over the country. This was, of course, welcome, but most of them were Young Liberals, and some of them were very liberal. Our headquarter became a lodging house for the volunteers, with them sleeping in all of the rooms, usually on the floor. The night-time parties became gradually wilder and, while to say there were orgies would be overstating, there were many liaisons taking place in public. The Liberal Party was, at that time, the only mainstream party actively campaigning for homosexual equality and so there were many gay men and lesbian women adding their variety of spice to the evenings. One of our helpers was Don Hale's son, Guy, then still in his teens. The HQ antics affected him so much that he accompanied me to church one Sunday so he 'could feel clean again'. The punch line to this is that he was, and still is, an ardent atheist.

Apart from the HQ shenanigans, there was much serious political work done, putting leaflets through as many doors as possible, radio and TV interviews and MP visits. Towards the end of the campaign with any kind of result slipping away from us, we organised a visit from Clement Freud, the MP from Ely. He was a well-known figure because of his TV appearance and his deep voice, usually used in a slow, deliberate way. This had proven very effective in a series of adverts for dog food! He was to come for an evening meeting in Stechford and a hall was booked and leaflets advertising the event delivered. Clem was known for not suffering fools and so when we got to the hall before him, we were worried. The audience consisted of just 6 people, one of whom had brought his dog! What would happen when the MP arrived? He strode through the door, looked at the assembled few, doubled by us volunteers and said, slowly, "Shall we all join hands and try and contact the living?"

The result was a disaster with us coming a distant fourth behind the National Front. The Conservatives won the seat but lost it back to Labour at the next General Election.

At about this time I and a young Liberal activist, Sarah Lewthwaite (daughter of our regional organiser) began to write and publish a regional newsletter, which we called "Black Beaver". With her father's regional responsivities Sarah was in a good position to get news and gossip and it rapidly became a rather juvenile, if amusing, satirical rag. It was all great fun until we wrote an expose of a senior local Liberal. It was, we thought, all made up and therefore, harmless. However, just before publication we found out that there was more than a grain of truth in our fiction, and we pulled the story to avoid ruining a good political career. Black Beaver didn't last long after that. Sarah Lewthwaite, however, went of to proper journalism and a career with the BBC.

One of the influential people behind the scenes in Birmingham liberalism was Sydney Caro. Sydney owned a badge making company and had bankrolled the party when it was almost extinct. I met him first when I went to my first National Assembly. Liberal Party Assemblies, usually held in a sea-side town, were the policy making body of the party, completely open to any member to attend, introduce motions and speak. They were also the opportunity to meet Liberals from all over the country and to enjoy ourselves in the evening. One of the most important parts of any Assembly are the fringe events, meetings outside the main hall and covering different interest groups and regions. Regional parties would hold their own get togethers, hiring meeting rooms and arranging caterers. Birmingham didn't run to this, ours was held in Sydney Caro's hotel room. It was there, sitting on a bed and drinking cheap wine, that I met David Luscombe, who was to become my closest political friend. He was an earnest young man who was certain that he would win a council seat in the Rotten Park ward. Two years later he was successful.

Three years later, in 1982, there were full council elections in Birmingham. I suppose I should explain the convoluted method used in Birmingham Council elections. Each year one third of the seats were contested, with successful candidates elected for a four-year period. Thus, in the fourth year, we were election free. This worked quite well until recently when we have gone for whole city elections every fourth year.

In 1982, we were all fighting on re-drawn boundaries and so every seat was up for grabs. I was one of three Liberal candidates in Brandwood and achieved my best ever result, getting 20.7% of the vote. However, across the whole city there were only four Liberals elected. Graham Gopsill and Steve Kirkham in Kingsbury and Dave Luscombe and Ken Hardeman in the new Ladywood seat. Hardeman was a strange man. He owned a successful city centre restaurant, The Celebrity, just off Broad Street in the city centre. Ken was on the far right of the liberal Party and he and I had many differences about policy. I have to say that whenever Lynn and I went to The Celebrity, we were treated royally, but in party meetings it was very different. By this time, I had been elected at the Chairman of the City Party. We were fighting elections alongside the SDP, which had been formed in March 1981. There was no formal agreement between the parties, but we had, informally agreed where each party would stand down. Hardeman did not like the SDP formed, as they were, by ex-Labour MPs. They were far too left wing for him and over the next year, he did all that he could to make sure that a proposed Alliance would never come to fruition. He lost that battle and lost his seat in 1983, a year when no Liberal or SDP candidate won a seat in Birmingham.

Things began to look better in the following year when we won 3 city seats. This also marked a change in approach, a move out of the city centre where seats were becoming more solidly Labour, and into the suburbs. The Alliance took Hall Green with a university lecturer and SDP member, Mick Wilkes and Yardley with Bill Doyle for the Liberals. Bill was a very special man and a rarity, a politician with no 'side'. If his feet were more solidly on the ground, they would have grown roots. He died far too soon and is missed.

The Alliance continued to make gains in the next two years seeing candidates elected who became huge parts of the Birmingham political scene. These included Ray Hassall, Neil Eustace and Paul Tilsley, all of whom will feature later in this chapter.

And so, we faced the 1987 General Election in good spirits. The Alliance was riding high in the polls and its leaders, David Owen for the SDP and David Steel for the Liberal Party, were popular with different areas of the electorate. The level of interest in the Alliance was brought home to me in October 1986 when, as Chief Agent, I was tasked with organising a Press Conference for David Steel and Shirley Williams. I booked a large room at the Grand Hotel and let the local press know. Liberal Party Head Office managed the national press. On the day, Lynn was working, and I had the care of Dunstan and Sadie then 12 and 10. So they came with me. When I got to the room, I had booked it was already crowded with both national and local press. TV cameras, a plethora of microphones and important guests. There was simply no room for a couple of kids. I moved my children to the bar, ordered them soft drinks, asked the barman to keep an eye on them, and went back to my Agent's duties. The conference went well, and I collected Dunstan and Sadie from the bar and put them in my car along with Shirley and David who I was transporting to Pebble Mill for a live interview with Ed Doolan on BBC Radio WM.

Shirley Williams, who was an absolute joy, remarked to the children that it must be quite a thrill meeting 'famous people'. Dunstan remarked that it was, he had seen Huey Lewis in the bar! (Huey Lewis and The News had played the Birmingham Odeon the night before. Shirley Williams was suitably chastened!

In preparation for the General Election, we set up an Alliance HQ in the city centre and began to work hard, daring to hope that we might win one seat in the City, Yardley where our local campaigns had had very positive results. As I had the previous year, I was charged with arranging a Party Leader Press Conference early in the campaign, this time for David Owen. I booked a larger room and made all the arrangements. I got there early to make sure everything was in order. It was and a little later I was joined by members of David Owen's staff team. They double checked everything, and it was obvious that they were in fear of him. Up until this time I had not met him, and, when I did, I wasn't impressed. He treated his team abominably, he was autocratic and, in my opinion, very self-centred.

As the election campaign went on the strategy of two parties with two leaders campaigning on the same Manifesto but travelling separately began to unravel. I saw this first hand when David Steel arrived to visit Yardley in his 'battle-bus'. I had arranged for Ed Doolan to do an interview with him in the bus and, while they were in the little studio at the back of the bus, I stayed in the main area where the travelling press were. They were busy calling their colleagues on the David Owen bus, telling them what Steel had said earlier and pushing for difference between to two leaders. There were differences, the two Davids could not agree on who they would support if there was a hung parliament among other things. We plummeted in the polls, and, in the Birmingham HQ, we were prepared for the poor results that we knew were on the cards. Those of us closely involved also realised that the only way forward was to merge the two parties into one. The result of the Election in October brought Margaret Thatcher back into power for the third time. It was time for a re-think.

Many within both parties shared my view that a merger was the only sensible way forward, but that didn't make it easy. Those opposed were passionate and the result was that we began with two parties and ended with three. The new Social and Liberal Democrats, and the continuing SDP, led by David Owen, and a small continuing Liberal Party. The Liberal Party held its final Assembly at the Norbreck Castle Hotel in Blackpool and I attended with Councillor David Luscombe. The majority to merge was large and I left with a feeling of being part of something important.

Initially, the new party had joint leaders, David Steel and Bob McClennan, until a suitable new leader could be elected. This would prove to be the beginning of my most active time politically.

The two candidates finally chosen to contest the leadership election were very different. Alan Beith was a traditional Liberal and appealed to that part of the membership that felt threatened by the influx of new, centrist and professional activists that came in with the SDP. I felt that voting for him would be voting for a return to the past and I wanted something different. That, I thought, is what Paddy Ashdown offered.

I had first noticed him at a fringe meeting some years before when he talked about the perils of 'short-term government'. This was a problem then and, unfortunately, is still a problem today. Because of our entrenched two-party system every government spends much of its time not planning for long-term reform but ensuring that it can win the next election. This has stifled innovation over the years, made important utilities like education, NHS and defence into political footballs, with superficial changes made whenever a new party came to power. He argued his case with passion and humour, and I was impressed so when it came to the leadership I was already committed. I wanted change, and that is what Paddy offered.

I offered to become part of his election team in Birmingham, circulating leaflets, speaking at meetings and doing whatever I could to help. The Birmingham hustings coincided with the birthday of Jane, Paddy's wife and so Paddy's office asked me to arrange a Chinese meal after the husting meeting to celebrate. Many of the Yeovil Liberal team had come up specially for this and I was honoured with an invitation. The restaurant was up-market Chinese, and the food and service were impeccable. Paddy had learned both Mandarin and Cantonese as an army interpreter and so, at the end of the meal, he thanked the main waiter in Mandarin. The waiter obviously did not understand so Paddy repeated the thanks in Cantonese, still to an obviously confused waiter. Then, in a moment of clarity, the waiter spoke, "Me no Chinese, me Vietnamese!". Cue much laughter at Paddy's expense, in which he joined.

Paddy's leadership coincided with my time as Birmingham Chief Agent and Regional Chair, so he was the leader with whom I had most contact. My recollections of those times were all positive. Paddy wasn't perfect, far from it, he had a ready temper and a sharp tongue. But he quickly forgot why he had been angry and moved on. He was good company, with a wealth of stories, some quite indiscreet. He had a good memory for people, possibly backed up by good briefings from his staff. He would bound out of his car like Tigger and boom "Blair, how are you?" across the car park.

Politically he was a sharp as the proverbial tack. He had a great ability to take in information and then re-use it later as if he had always known it. This could be really useful in public meetings. I recall one such meeting in a Birmingham constituency, close to the constituency boundary of another MP. There is an understanding that if a sitting MP is visiting another constituency to speak, the visitor will inform the local MP as a courtesy. This meeting was in Hall Green, and we had informed the local MP, the Conservative Andrew Hargreaves. However, just before Paddy arrived, I got wind that the MP for Selly Oak, Labour's Lynne Jones, was in our audience and that she was to challenge Paddy because she thought we were in her constituency. When Paddy arrived, I told him about this as we walked from the car and told him that we were not in her constituency which began about 150 yards from our meeting. After he had made his speech, Lynne Jones did challenge him for his lack of courtesy in informing her of his visit. Paddy looked confused, hurt even. He apologised for any oversight but said he was sure that her constituency boundary was over a hundred yards away and named the road I had told him. It was her turn to be confused now and she turned to her agent whose face grew red as he realised that this incomer from Devon seemed to know more about the political map of Birmingham than he did. Game, set and match to Paddy.

Paddy had another rare attribute for a leader, he listened and appeared genuinely interested in your opinions and ideas. He had begun as a member of the Labour Party and I believe that if he had stayed there, he would have reached cabinet status. However, he truly believed that we needed a realignment of British politics and that would never come from Labour or the Conservatives.

There are many other politicians I have met that have impressed and influenced me but, rather than trying to shoehorn them into a time-based narrative, I thought I would attempt some brief pen-pictures.

David Penhaligon was a Cornishman and Liberal MP for Truro where he had led the local Young Liberals. He was a passionate West Country man, and one of the first proponents of the, "If you have something to say, put it in a leaflet and shove it through doors", political strategy. This not only won him his seat but was followed by Liberals all over the country and changed the way that we 'did' politics. He was a remarkably humble man, which is unusual in MPs! I hosted him in Birmingham when he came, as the Liberal Party Transport spokesman, to look at the new Birmingham Airport. Having him with me for some time, I also got him, reluctantly, to do an open-air speech from a truck outside Birmingham Cathedral. We arrived early and none of my local Liberal contacts were there. David got out of the car muttering, "I don't know why I'm here; no bugger knows me outside Cornwall". Almost as soon as his feet hit the pavement, a passer-by said, "Nice to see you Mr Penhaligon". He was convinced that I had set this up, even as the man walked away, not to be seen again.

He died in a car crash on December 22nd, 1986, driving on icy roads doing constituency visits. I firmly believe that he would have been in the running for the next leader because of his popularity across the whole party.

Of course, the people I knew best in politics were those in my local area. Within the Liberal Party and its successor, there have been many who really made an impact on me. I have mentioned Bill Doyle before but there were many others. Sydney Caro, a local businessman who, almost single-handedly, kept the Liberal Party alive during the dark days where there was almost no electoral success in Birmingham. John Hemming, another Birmingham businessman, who was one of those that led the LibDem assault on the Yardley area.

He was assisted in his elevation by the work of another Councillor, Neil Eustace, who also served as John's agent. Neil was just the best organiser I ever met. He didn't suffer fools, expected everyone to work as hard as he did, and was successful. In many ways, it was his organisation that enable us to win all nine council seats in the Yardley constituency and then hold on to them.

Paul Tilsley MBE was another of those to benefit from Neil Eustace's expertise. He first won his Sheldon seat in 1987 and, as I write this, he still holds it, making him the longest serving councillor in Birmingham. He had previously held an inner-city ward, so his activity in Liberal politics goes back well over 50 years. In 1993 he became the first Liberal Lord Mayor of Birmingham for over forty years. I was fortunate to be at the Mayor making ceremony, sitting next to Sidney Caro, who was in tears. After the barren years he was now witnessing a Liberal milestone. Over the years I got to know Paul well and, although we do not always agree, I hold him in great esteem. He is passionate about his politics and has achieved a great deal in his time. During a period when we had a 'hung' council, Paul served as deputy leader of the council with distinction. In my opinion, he was far more able than the Conservative leader!

John Hemmings is a Birmingham businessman who also became a councillor in the Yardley area and became the leader of the council group of Liberal Democrats. Although I remember him in his student days, he rapidly became successful in his computer business, writing bespoke programs mainly for the legal profession. His success brought him wealth and by the time he became a councillor, he was a millionaire. His money enabled him to bankroll his local party and maintain an office in Yardley and pay staff. This, combined with his determination helped him to become the only Birmingham Liberal Democrat elected to Parliament in my political lifetime. John was an able MP but, in my mind, he had one major disadvantage. His personal skills were not the best. He has no time for small talk, always wanting to get to the main business without delay. This can make him appear cold and aloof, which I don't think he is, but in politics impressions count. He won the Yardley constituency seat in the General Election in 2005, held it with an increased majority in 2010. He lost the seat to the charismatic Labour candidate, Jess Phillips in 2015.

Jim Whorwood, along with Ian Powney, sent shockwaves through local politics when they broke the Conservative stranglehold in Sutton Coldfield, winning two seats on the now defunct West

Midland County Council. Later he joined the exodus to Yardley, becoming a city councillor in Acocks Green ward in 1997. He became Lord Mayor in 2001 when the Labour and Liberal Group came together to reject the Conservative nomination of John Lines. (John Lines was on the right of his party and regarded with much suspicion by many councillors. However, when became the council cabinet lead for housing, he became a great supporter of St. Basils). Jim Whorwood also became convinced of the value of St Basils when he visited during his Mayoralty and, thereafter, donated all of his earnings from speaking engagements to our charity. Jim was Mayor at the time of 9/11 and travelled to New York on behalf of Birmingham to express both condolences and support. He spent many of his later years restoring a 1930 Austin Seven box saloon car and when he died in 2023 there was a wonderful floral tribute in the shape of that car. It was always a pleasure to be in Jim's company.

David Luscombe was and is my closest Liberal friend. I have already told of how I met him at my first Liberal Party Assembly, he impressed me then, and he continues to do so 50 years later. Although he was a supporter of the coming together of the two parties, I think he would consider himself as on the Liberal wing of the LibDems. With due deference to others who held the post, he was the best local party leader that I worked with. He was leader in the difficult years when the party in local government was very small. The party office in those days was in the Council House basement, opposite the Gentlemen's toilets, and the whiff would occasionally cross the corridor. Small we may have been but, under David's leadership, we were always responsible. I remember many hours sitting with David in that room, putting together Manifestos for local government elections, always properly costed with the City treasurer. David then, and now, takes his politics seriously.

He, like me, spent many years working for a local charity, an expression of his commitment to social justice which also fired his politics. After a break from front line council politics, David returned for some years as a political advisor for the LibDem council group, advising on policy development.

This is not the place for personal revelations, but I have to mention that since 1986 David has battled a degenerative disease which he has faced with the same determination that he demonstrated in every part of his life.

Politics is a much-maligned profession these days as we hear stories of sleaze, corruption and broken promises. For many people this has led to the feeling that 'They are all the same' or 'They are all in for themselves'. This has not been my experience of the last half century. I have been impressed by the majority of politicians, local and national, that I have met and worked with. Inspired with a desire to make things better, they dedicated themselves to doing that in the way that they thought best. Many times, I disagreed with their methods, but I could appreciate the motivation. I live in hope that, in time, we will return to an appreciation of public service.

CHAPTER 11 - ST BASILS – EARLY YEARS

In 1994 I went to a party at the house of my cousin Jean. Jean was married to the Rev Les Milner who, I knew, was the managing director of a charity called St Basils. They worked with young homeless people in Birmingham but that was about all I knew of them. During a conversation I mentioned that I was looking for a job and Les said that there was a position that would be advertised soon in their fundraising department. He offered to let me know when the advert was placed made clear that that was as far as he would go with helping me.

A few weeks later, the advert was placed, and I got the job description. They were looking for someone to join the fundraising department specifically to take over responsibility for contact with schools and faith organisations as well as more general fundraising. As I read the job description, I realised that it was a perfect fit for me. I had all the attributes that they required, and, though I had no experience in fundraising, my background in sales and marketing would be ideal for the position. The only problem was the salary. This was considerably lower than I had been used to, but I thought that, should I get the job, it would look good on my CV when moving on. I did get the job and accepted it but, in the back of my mind, I really only intended to stay for 18 months or so until a better paid position was available.

My starting date was Thursday, 16 June and it started quite amusingly. Three weeks previously there had been local elections in Birmingham, and I have been a guest on behalf of the Liberal party in the election broadcast on BBC West Midlands radio. During the evening Dennis Minnis was elected as a Labour councillor. Interestingly, he had been the leader of the Liberal party in Birmingham at the time that I joined some 20 years before. He had resigned from the Liberal party and joined the Labour Party, and this was his political comeback. Of course, Ed Doolan, the host of the programme, knew this and, therefore, came to be me first for comment. I said that I welcomed Dennis back to the Council House noting that "the Liberal party had taught him everything he knows about politics!"

Forward to my first morning at St Basils. I'm sitting in the entrance hall waiting for my new boss to come and greet me when who should walk through the doors but Councillor Dennis Minnis. I had forgotten that he worked for St Basils as head of the drop-in centre, The Link. He looked at me and quoted, "Taught me everything I know, did you?". My embarrassment was quickly ended as David Goss, Head of Fundraising, came in and rescued me.

I joined a tight little team in fundraising. It consisted of David Goss, our leader, Suki Sahota, our secretary, and a lady who looked after applications to charitable trusts, whose name I have unforgivably forgotten. The office also included our press and publicity officer, Cathy Clarke. Cathy was extremely deaf, and, at the beginning, I found her intimidating. Because of her hearing impairment you had to remember to look at her when you spoke, and if you didn't, she would remind you quite forcefully. However, in time she became a good friend as well as a colleague.

I had been employed to head up approaches to schools and educational organisations as well as taking over the responsibility for churches and faith organisations from Les Milner. I would, of course, be involved in all other aspects of our fundraising efforts.

David Goss was brilliant to work for. He was able to bring out and encourage the best in all of us and in my case, he quickly spotted my abilities for public speaking. Within six months of my appointment, he was giving me the responsibility for leading meetings because he thought that I did it better than he did. This takes a great deal of self-confidence from the manager and David had that in great measure. He had held a senior management position at Boots in Nottingham prior to moving to Birmingham after his marriage had broken down. After joining St Basils, he threw himself wholeheartedly into the charity sector using every bit of his management skill to improve our connection with the business sector.

I, too, threw myself into my new responsibilities. Church contacts I found quite easy; my interdenominational background made me feel comfortable with any church. I found myself preaching in Anglican churches as well as nonconformist and, occasionally, Roman Catholic. Schools, however, were a different area and one that I had no real knowledge of. So, I called upon the expertise of my cousin Anne who was, at that time, head of Waverley school. She invited me into her school where we had a very productive chat about how I could leverage help from schools and their pupils.

One of the things that I discovered very early in my career at St Basils was how normal our residents were. They were nothing like most people's preconceptions of homeless young people and so, as I got to know some of them, I would invite them to come with me to schools to address classes or assemblies. The schoolchildren would, almost always, assume that the young person with me was an assistant, until I got them to tell their stories. This was always revelation and drew an understanding response from the young audiences. Support from schools went up exponentially in a very short time.

I quickly got to love my new job, but in my mind, it was still really only temporary. The pay was not good enough, but I found myself more and more involved. The hours, as well, were undefinable. You had to be available when the prospective funder wanted you to be available. This could involve speaking at a Rotary Club meeting on Wednesday night or leading three services at Henley in Arden Parish Church on Sunday. Needless to say, there was no overtime pay, but we were encouraged to take off time in lieu and, over the years, I learnt that that was a very sensible thing to do.

I suppose my attitude to continuing with the job came one morning when I met Les Milner at the coffee bar in the front of the church. I was making myself a cup and obviously offered to make him one too. As we waited for the kettle I told him, rather excitedly, about a recent successful meeting I had. He looked at me and said, "You do realise, Blair, that this is your calling?". I responded with scorn, but looking back, he was right. I was hooked. For the first time in my professional career, I was using all the skills that I had gathered in salesmanship, politics, public speaking and finance, all for one good cause that was making a difference in my city.

Over the next few years, I continued with the same job description but with a growing number of ad hoc responsibilities. I was fronting for the organisation in many places including on local radio and being instrumental in organising events. There were minor staff changes in the Department, but the majority continued, and we were in good, tight, team.

There was however a problem. The organisation was always running on a shoestring. The grants that we got from the local government were slowly phased out and replaced with contracts that we had to bid for. Les never stopped having ambitions and so we were always incurring extra expenditure, both capital and running costs. Our properties always needed maintenance and there were great plans for a new property in Bordesley Green. This development would contain a range of self-contained flats ranging from one-bedroom to family units. Each would have its own kitchen and bathroom and be completely self-contained. It would cost a fortune to build, and a lot more to run. Fortunately, Les had involved Mark and Barbara Edmonds. Mark ran a company that was approaching a major milestone and had put aside money to mark the anniversary. My memory, unreliable, tells me that the total amount that we had from the Edmonds was £56,000. The property was named "Edmonds Court". It rapidly became my "go to" place when I had to show visitors a project. It was run by a wonderful, charismatic lady called Jennifer Johnson who never failed to make an impression on potential funders. The premises themselves were of high quality.

Going to Edmonds Court was a quick and easy way to show people that we thought that our residents deserved a good standard of accommodation and, that giving them that standard would give them something to aspire to when they left St Basils.

For myself, over the years my salary rose little by little, but more to the point, I was enjoying going to work every day.

I could write a whole book about my time at St Basils, so I shall just pick out a few highlights and maybe a couple of low lights.

In September 1995 the television show "Challenge Anneka" came calling. The challenge that they set themselves was to convert a property we have just obtained into accommodation for young people with the usual facilities including office space. The challenge, as usual, was to complete in three days. They set up their headquarters in a pub car park opposite our property and set to work. For those three days my entire time was spent supporting them. This included speaking at a reception for the team that had gathered. This led to a relatively rare letter of congratulations from Les in which he said, "thank you so much for making everybody feel welcome, for giving them information, encouraging them, and generally selling "St Basils" so well."

The only problem was that the challenge "failed" but the good news was that the contractors came back and finish the job later. I really enjoyed being "on set" with the TV production crew but, by far, the best thing about it was the catering truck! As this was an ongoing challenge it was providing food for 24 hours a day, and good quality food at that. The production team were friendly and accommodating although Miss Rice herself was rather distant.

The biggest new event that we introduced was the St Basils walk. The first of these took place on 20 June 1998 and, as I write, the event still continues over 25 years later. The idea came from Nick Venning who was chair of our Fundraising Committee. This was a group of interested businesspeople, church leaders and other concerned parties, who met regularly to advise the fundraising team. Nick himself was an enormous support to me throughout my time at the charity and I owe him a great deal.

The first walk was actually entitled the "St Basils Yomp". It was based on SAS training and the challenge for our entrance was to walk from Okehampton to Ivybridge across Dartmoor, a walk of over 30 miles on rough country. Part of the challenge was for the teams to plan their own route; we gave them only one stipulation that they had to pass through Princetown and then check-in at our base in Ivybridge before going home. Surprisingly, there were a number of companies and groups that took up this challenge, and it was successful enough for us to attempt it the following year. That second try was almost a disaster.

Firstly, the weather. It rained throughout most of the day, mist set in, what had been streams became rivers but we, perhaps foolishly, decided to go ahead. Looking back, we were lucky. Nobody got injured and, eventually, we got everybody home. It was a lesson learned and, thereafter, we selected circular routes, with numerous checkpoints so that we can keep track of the contestants and ensure their safety. Year after year the number of teams increased, and we began offering shorter routes. With Nick Venning and Steve Rainbow doing the legwork we were able to present new routes for every year. This made every year a different challenge which brought people back time after time. We adapted to attract more teams. Still offering the long walk at approximately 25 miles, we added a shorter, 13-mile, course. Over time this event became one of the major fundraisers in the calendar, and, though challenging to organise, one of the best experiences. For many years the responsibility of organising fell to Michael Norris who did a brilliant job.

1998 saw another milestone in my lay preaching, my first funeral. Lynn's aunt Connie, who had raised seven children in a three bedroomed house in Sparkhill had moved out to Redditch and was happy and settled there. Tragedy struck when she died suddenly and without warning. The family approached me and asked if I would conduct the funeral, at Yardley Crematorium. I was in a quandary, and the truth was, I didn't want to do it. I went to see my friend

Graham Spicer, a minister in the United Reformed Church. I told him what had been asked and how I felt, hoping that he would offer to step in and take the service. Instead, he offered me these words, "You do know that conducting a funeral is the last act of love that you can do for someone on this earth?". He had me cornered, how could I say no? So, I said yes. Graham helped me with all the preparation, gave me suggested content and advised me on how to talk to the relatives to get the stories that they wanted at the funeral. He stressed that this should be a celebration of a life, not centred on the death, but on the life that had been lived. More than 25 years later I have conducted dozens of funerals and always stuck to the principles that Graham instilled in me back then.

Sleepout was the other big fundraising event. This had begun well before I had joined the organisation and was the brainchild of Cathy Clarke who continue to run it for many years. The idea was simple, we challenge people to sleep for one night on the street, with nothing but cardboard for their bed. They get sponsored to do this and they get a small experience of what it is like for those who have no choice but to sleep rough in our big cities. Of course, it isn't a real experience. Come the dawn they get up, go home, and have a good breakfast and shower. Real rough sleepers don't have that possibility.

The truth is that, in my early days I wasn't keen on the sleepout. The only one I attended was outside St Martin's in the Bullring. It upset a genuine rough sleeper who normally slept in that location, and it was disrupted by noisy revellers going home who found it fun to kick down the cardboard dwellings as they passed. I decided to opt out and start a complimentary event on the same night. This would be a vigil where churches would host an overnight event with prayers on each hour for those really suffering from homelessness. We managed to get the approval and involvement of the cathedral and a number of churches throughout the city. While local clergy did the majority of the work, Les and I tried to do at least one of the hourly section. Though this event only lasted a few years, it did result in solidifying our relations with a many churches and their congregations across the city.

Later, when I became Head of Fundraising, I brought the Sleepout to Heathmill Lane, and the St Basils car park where it was easier to put in security and use the facilities at the centre.

By 1998, I was a well-established member of the fundraising team and enjoying the different challenges that every week threw up. However, change was in the air. Les decided that he needed more support at management level and promoted David Goss to Deputy Managing Director. This meant, of course, that there was a vacancy for Head of Fundraising. After much deliberation, I decided to apply going through a rigorous interview procedure. I eventually made the final two but lost out at the final hurdle to Claire Cassidy who was appointed to the post in April 1998. Like all new appointees, she had her own ideas and agenda and there were many changes for us to content with.

Her first, and major, change was to begin a cost benefit control on all of us. This involved keeping detailed timesheets of the times we spent on different endeavours together with the financial benefits therefrom. This was very difficult for my station. Schools and churches would never bring in as much money as Charitable Trusts, the area run by Michael Norris. Financially there was no comparison, but I always felt that my efforts raised much more awareness of youth homelessness than almost anything else that we did. The job, always stressful, became really difficult.

By August it was becoming almost intolerable. I became irritable, short tempered and constantly stressed. I continued to fulfil my obligations, but it became harder and harder. Then I began to have physical symptoms. My hair began to fall out in clumps, and I was diagnosed with stress alopecia. I have to say at this point that Claire and the St Basils HR team were very supportive. They found, and paid for, a therapist to help me deal with my stress and gave me some time off to recover. The therapist was brilliant, and I still use some of his methods today to cope with any pressure that may come along. The hair loss, in fact, added to the stress. My head looked like a badly designed chessboard with growing holes showing a bare scalp beneath. Eventually I decided to take control and shaved my whole head. I have now been completely bald for over 25 years with no regrets.

Most of my experiences at St Basils were positive but in January 1999 that changed. Claire approached me and shared concerns that she had had about the appointment system that we had both gone through. She asked me for my impressions and, in general, they reflected hers. She just asked me to write them down and include them in a submission to HR about the procedure. I did so very carefully, conscious of the fact that anything I said could be seen as coming from the viewpoint of a disappointed candidate. A little while later I was summoned by the managing director and accused of undermining Claire Cassidy. I was devastated, I could not understand how Les Milner could even contemplate that I would do such a thing. Although I pleaded my innocence the effect of this debacle took away my pleasure from the job for many months thereafter.

Claire's management style was very different from her predecessor, much more confrontational and this led to the team becoming factionalised. There were those, like Meredith Davison, who felt that Claire was a breath of fresh air. There were others, like Cathy Clarke, who found the new regime oppressive and counterproductive. I tended towards the latter but was determined, no matter what Les may have thought, to give Claire the benefit of the doubt and do my best to support her.

However, as the year went on, her methods and her attitude were beginning to alienate senior management as well as some of her team. Eventually in August 2000 she was relieved of her duties. David Goss took overall charge of the Department and asked me if I would become interim manager until the post could be filled. Having been rejected before I had no intention to put myself forward for the newly vacant post and therefore refused the interim position which was then given to Michael Norris.

Not certain of my future I applied for the position of Secretary to the Bishop of Birmingham. I went through the interview procedures and was eventually one of two shortlisted for the post. At this point, David Goss was asked for a reference by the Bishop's office. His last paragraph of this reference, copied to me, changed my mind about my position.

It read, "Should Blair be appointed to this vacancy, or leave St Basils for any other reason, and then express a wish to return to this employment, I would have no hesitation in recommending his possible reemployment in the role that he has occupied for the last six years." The confidence that David expressed in me made me rethink my position and I withdrew from the interview procedure at the Bishop's office.

I returned to my fundraising activities with greater enthusiasm and, coupled with changes at the very top of our organisation, began to reassess my future.

It was also about this time that Les Milner decided the right time had come to retire. He had talked to me about this two years previously but made the decision to stay on. In retrospect I feel that it would have been better for him and his family for him to have left when he was first thinking about it but, hindsight is always perfect vision.

With the announcement that he was going, the search for his successor began. Of course, those of us not involved had no idea how the process was progressing but eventually the decision was made. The new Managing Director of St Basils would be Jean Templeton, who had over 20 years' experience of managing housing and neighbourhood services in a number of Local Authorities in the Northeast and Midlands. Just after her appointment was released, I discovered she was speaking at a meeting at the Midlands Arts Centre. I got myself invited and went to see what the new boss was going to be like. I was not impressed. In fact, I came home and told Lynn that "she would not last six months". As I write this in January 2024 she has completed 23 years in the post.

At first, she and Les worked alongside each other for a handover period. Although I can't be sure, I don't think that this was very successful because they both had different visions for the organisation.

It was during this time that the post of Head of Fundraising was advertised. Michael Norris, who had been making a decent fist of running the Department applied immediately. After my disappointment when I first applied for the role, I had determined that I would not go for it again. However, a number of people, including David Goss, thought that I should and, eventually, I put my name forward without a great deal of enthusiasm.

It may have been that because of this I was more relaxed about the interview procedures and sailed through them. By the time that I was appointed to the role on 20 March 2001, Les had left, and it was Jean who welcomed me to the new role.

CHAPTER 12 - US AND THE USA

November 2000 saw us go on our first holiday to the United States. Specifically, to Orlando in Florida.

We started planning it almost a year in advance with our friends Cheryl and Ken Plant and Rita and Graham Spicer. The idea was to spend two weeks visiting Disney and the NASA Space Centre. Lynn was not as keen on 'visiting the Mouse' as the rest of us. It was not her ideal holiday and she thought that it was somewhat childish. We won her over by promising her that, in the middle of the holiday, we would move for a couple of days to the coast on the Gulf of Mexico, for some 'beach time'.

We flew from Birmingham to Newark, where we would change planes and fly onto Orlando Airport. This would be, of course, my longest flight and, as such, filled me with foreboding. Then, and now, I didn't enjoy flying. For Lynn the holiday starts when we leave home, for me it begins when I am finally off the plane! However, you have to temper your fear with some commonsense, and so I do fly, but without enjoyment. On this occasion the first part of the journey went well, and we arrived in Newark with plenty of time to make the transfer. There was a little delay in loading the Orlando flight, and on board we settled into our seats. Then, nothing happened. We just sat there. For a long time. My anxiety levels grew. Eventually they told is that there was a slight problem with the aircraft and that we would be 'de-planed' and given some food vouchers while we waited.

We waited some hours before we were called back to embark, and my friends were very supportive with my fears. Of course, the flight was fine, but the delays meant that we arrived in Orlando very late at night and were the last into the Alamo Car Hire to collect our vehicle. The clerk, a huge Afro-American, beamed at us and bellowed across the hall, "Where have you been? We have been so worried!".

Luggage loaded into the vehicle we set off to find our villa, situated some miles away in Kissimmee. No Satnav, but we had Rita. With only a road map she gave precise instructions to our driver, Ken, and we found the estate first time! Impressed with her abilities I have named all my Satnavs 'Rita' ever since.

However, in the dark, all of the rentals looked alike, and we almost broke into someone else's place before located our home for the next two weeks. The next morning, we started our American adventure with breakfast at Dennys, a popular restaurant chain. When I look back now, I can see that there would have been many better places to enjoy breakfast, but we were new, and we had seen Dennys on TV! I showed off by being the only one to understand the waitress when she asked how we wanted our eggs. (Over easy in my case). The waitress also charmed me when Ken asked what were 'grits'? She gave him the advice that, "Sir, you don't want grits!". Having subsequently tried them, she was right.

Full of greasy carbohydrates, we made our way to Disney. Ken had done all the planning for this, and he had worked out that it was easier to drive to Epcot and take the monorail to The Magic Kingdom. All of Lynn's reservations disappeared as we looked down 'Main Street' and the grin didn't leave her face all day. There is no doubt in my mind that the Americans do theme parks extremely well. It isn't just the rides, good though they are, it is the storytelling around the rides and attractions.

In our two weeks we visited Magic Kingdom, Epcot, Hollywood Studios and Blizzard Beach, a Disney water park. My favourite was Epcot, less frenetic than the other parks, with a huge lake to walk around with 'towns', representing countries from around the world. Of course, the UK was represented by thatched cottages, a pub, a fish and chip shop and red telephone boxes and pillar boxes. Epcot was supposed to be Walt Disney's view of the future and I found it entrancing. It also featured the greatest firework display that I had ever seen, across the lake. That night we booked into one of the lakeside restaurants, so we only had to wander out from our table to view the display.

We also visited the newer Universal Studio theme park, which was to become my favourite place. It was separated into two areas, one was almost like an extended film set and the other, called the Islands of Adventure, had different themed areas with rides and experience that fitted the theme. All of them were state-of-the art, with amazing graphics and effects. Some were literally all encompassing, putting you at the heart of the action. My geekiness was satisfied!

NASA, a drive away from Orlando, was a day trip that was more than worthwhile. The history of American spaceflight was here, and many of the displays features items that were not reproductions but had really been involved in the efforts to place a man on the moon. For example, one of the actual Gemini spacecraft that had been piloted by astronauts Virgil "Gus" Grissom and John Young. The heat shield showed how tight the margins were on re-entry. In some places it was burnt through almost to the metal beneath.

The sight of the Saturn V launch rocket was breathtaking, there is no way of knowing how big it is until you stand next to it, and the graveyard of rockets showed the progress that had been made over the decades. NASA is situated in a protected nature reserve and so it was quite interesting to see huge alligators in the waterways around the site.

The middle weekend came and so we left our rental and drove off West, aiming for the Gulf of Mexico. We ended up in Anna Maria Island. A small island, connected to the mainland with three bridges, Anna Maria became our favourite place in the word. It is hard to describe the charm of the place, but some of it may have to do with a local ordinance that says that nothing built on the island can be taller than the tallest tree. So, no high-rise hotels, no huge shopping malls, just locally owned, shops, motels and restaurants. We booked into The White Sands Motel. Lynn and I had one room, while the others shared a larger room. This was our first experience of motel rooms with not just a bed and a bathroom, but a fitted kitchen as well. These, we discovered, were called 'Efficiencies'.

The beach, literally two minutes from our room, was white sand, the weather was wonderful, and we chilled after our theme park exertions. On our first night there we went to local, upmarket, fish restaurant called Lavroches. We ordered our starters and the waitress asked if we would like bread with that. We said yes and she arrived with four loaves for six people. Americans eat big!

The next morning, we found a breakfast restaurant right on the beach and enjoyed our food in the glorious Floridian sunshine. One of the offers was an 'all you can eat' pancake breakfast, which Lynn opted for. Having eaten her first stack, she returned to the pancake stand and asked for two more. "Two?", questioned the cook. "Two? Don't you like my pancakes?". Americans eat big!

After three days we returned to our base in Orlando and continued to enjoy what the theme parks had to offer. It was a glorious holiday, spent with great friends and, although Lynn and I had thought that this would be a one-off American holiday, we left determined to return, especially to Anna Maria.

In the event, that didn't take long. In fact, just 12 months later we were boarding a flight from Birmingham to Newark where this time we would transfer to a flight bound for Tampa, some miles north of Anna Maria Island. All went well and we spent our first night in a motel in Tampa having collected our hire car. The next morning, we drove over a spectacular bridge to Anna Maria and back to the White Sands Motel.

We were not disappointed. On our own we explored all that the island had to offer and the local city of Sarasota. One evening we went to a dinner theatre in Sarasota to see the musical Nunsense2. Whilst it was completely nonsensical it was a great experience combining theatre and food, two of my very favourite things. We also took the opportunity to revisit St Petersburg and the great Salvador Dali Museum. This houses the greatest collection of Dali's works in the world. I had gone there with Graham Spicer the previous year, but this time I was able to spend longer and see more. In St Petersburg we also visited a museum which had a display regarding the Cuban crisis and how Pres Kennedy had handled it. It was very sobering to see how close the world had come to nuclear war at that time and how the president had had to stand up to his military advisers to avoid conflict. We also took the time to visit the Myakka State National Park, with a boat trip to see the wildlife including many alligators.

The end of the holiday came with us returning to Tampa to join our flight. The desk clerk was confused, she was able to book us on to the flight from Tampa to Newark but for some reason not on the plane from Newark to Birmingham. She advised us to check in again at Newark. This we did to find there was a problem. It was explained to us that there had been weather delays in the north of America which meant that many passengers were now on standby for flights out of Newark, including ours. However, they were able to get us onto our flight, but we would not be able to sit together. As I have mentioned before, I am a nervous flyer and the thought of not being next to Lynn was difficult to accept. We asked if there was any alternative. The suggestion was that when called to the gate we should ask the attendants there if they could do anything about it.

When the time came this is what we did but, very politely, we were informed that they could not change the seat allocations. "In that case, I don't think I am able to fly.", I said. There was a conversation between the staff members. "We have a number of passengers on standby for this flight. If you were prepared to give up your seats, we promise to fly you out on the same plane tomorrow, sitting together, and we will put you up in a hotel overnight." At that point, I would have been happy to say a resounding yes, but the airline representative continued, "we will also give you $750 in vouchers." This was a win-win situation and very soon we set found ourselves in a coach on the way to a Holiday Inn.

The next day we found ourselves with hours to fill before we needed to go back to the airport and so we had a day in New York. We took the train from Newark to Pennsylvania Station and then took the New York bus tour. It would have been ideal, but this was November, and we were dressed for sunny Florida. My photographs at the end of the tour are all blurred because of the way I was shivering. But that day New York was absolute bonus. We made our way back to Newark and checked in to find that everything was in order and that the vouchers promised were for $750 each! One catch, they had to be used within 12 months. It looked like we would be coming back to the US sooner than we expected.

Knowing that we "had" to return to the USA in 2004 put me into a frenzy of organisation. Where would we go? The United States is huge and there were a large number of places that were on my bucket list (which only existed in my head). For me, part of the joy of any holiday is the planning, and I really enjoyed this. Rather than just being a holiday, this would be an adventure.

Firstly, we flew to Las Vegas, a place that I had always dreamt of going to. Truth is that this was not Lynn's first choice, but that would be made up to her with the rest of the places I had planned for us to go. First impression of Las Vegas was exactly what I expected, with slot machines in the reception area of the airport! We made our way to our hotel, The Orleans, which was a mid-range hotel off the main strip. It is one of the smaller hotels in Las Vegas but was still the biggest hotel that we had ever been in. It had a cinema, bowling alley, theatre, swimming pools and a plethora of restaurants, completed, of course, by a huge casino. We checked in and, tired from our journeys, collapsed into our huge queen size bed.

The time difference meant that we awoke at 4 AM, Las Vegas time, but this was not a problem. At 4:30 we were sat in a restaurant enjoying a full breakfast. Nothing is ever closed in Las Vegas. We spent our first day exploring and finding out that every hotel/casino has its own story to tell. Paris Las Vegas has a replica Arc de Triomphe and Eiffel Tower outside and, inside, boulevards with bistros. The Venetian has a canal that runs from outside through the building into a reproduction of St Mark Square. The attention to detail is amazing and, while we were visiting, we were entertained by a group of opera singers on the bandstand in the square. New York, New York features a typical New York St with gratings issuing steam from the subway, which doesn't exist! It also has a rollercoaster that runs in and out of the building. The great thing is you don't have to pay to go into any of these attractions, they just hope that you will end up in the casino.

That first night we went to a show which I had pre-booked back in England. It starred a number of singing groups such as The Coasters, The Platters and The Drifters. This show was in the Sahara hotel at the far end of The Strip, and we travelled there by public transport. The show was excellent although not many of the groups featured their original lineups!

The next big discovery was the half-price ticket office which, in the morning, offered cut-price admission to shows during the day. In fact, one of the lunchtime shows we went to featured a top ventriloquist, Ronn Lucas, and the tickets were free as long as you bought at least one drink each. We caught a number of shows over the three days that we were there but, for me, the highlight was the Star Trek Experience at the Las Vegas Hilton.

This began with a display of artefacts from the series from Star Trek, The Next Generation, Deep Space Nine and Voyager. This was billed as the largest collection in the world, and I can believe it. Then we joined the experience. A group of about 12 of us were ushered into a 'lift', supposedly to take us to the next part of the exhibition, but, as the lift started to move. The lights went out, there was a swooshing noise and, when the lights returned, we were on the command deck of the USS Enterprise!

As other crewmembers worked around us, Commander Riker greeted us from the main screen telling us that they had beamed us aboard from the past because the Klingons were going to kill us all, as one of us might be an ancestor of Captain Pickard and eliminating us might mean he was never born! A wonderfully preposterous idea, but it opened us up to adventures as we moved about the ship for the next 20 minutes. After drinks in a space bar, we transferred to another adventure where we chased down corridors by the Borg, evacuated in a shuttle, attacked in space and finally rescued by Captain Janeway.

I realise that little of this will make sense to readers who are not Trekkies, but it was amazing and exciting to experience. The realism of the sets and the brilliance of the effects made it all almost believable.

After three nights in Vegas, we were off on the next part of our adventure. Picking up a hire car, we drove to Zion National Park, Utah. This is a 160-mile drive, and we arrived late afternoon in Springdale, where we stayed at the Bumbleberry Motel. Having left the sunshine of Las Vegas behind, we arrived in pouring rain. Mentioning this to the lady on reception, she told me to consider myself lucky, following rain we would see sights that weren't there when the weather was good. She was right, the following day there was a waterfall that doesn't exist in the dry.

Zion is renowned for its massive sandstone cliffs that come alive in hues of cream, pink, and red. These towering formations create a dramatic landscape against the brilliant blue sky. It was unlike anything we had seen before, and we were also impressed with the care that was taken to maintain the park in a pristine state. You could not drive into the park, you had to use the parks own shuttle buses to take you to the beginning of your walk to the Canyon. Unlike the Grand Canyon (more later) Zion is experienced from the floor of the canyon. You can walk alongside the river and see both the views and the wildlife. On our second day, we got more adventurous and went on a solo hike that took us through wonderful scenery with rivers, mountains, waterfalls and more. To attempt this, we both had to buy proper footwear and we bought quality. Lynn's lasted into 2023 and mine, less used, are still going strong.

Springdale was a very small town, mainly catering for the tourists. In my research back at home, I had discovered that they had a small theatre, The Bumbleberry Theatre, next to our motel. Better still, at the time we would be there they were featuring a Rock and Roll review. I booked it, knowing that it would be a small-town production, little better than amateur. I was wrong, the only thing small about it was the theatre itself, the production was very impressive with an enthusiastic cast, only one of who was old enough to remember the rock n roll era!

Our next destination was the big one, The Grand Canyon. At that time of year, late October, I had been warned that the route around the North end of the Canyon might be unsafe because of snow, so I had intended to drive back around Las Vegas and then approach the other side of the Canyon. However, having checked the weather whilst in Springdale, the shorter route was still open, so that is the way we went. I hadn't made any reservation for the overnight stop we would have to make but felt confident that we would find somewhere. The total journey is around 255 miles which, in the UK, would be a long trip. In America it is just a short hop. It is difficult to get our minds about how vast the US is, I now understand why most Americans never leave their country. Why should they? It has every kind of location that you could possibly want.

In fact, we stayed in a little town called Page in Coconino County, Arizona. Having checked in to a motel, we went into the centre of the town and booked ourselves on a visit to Antelope Canyon, a slot canyon on Navajo land east of the town. The journey there was the problem, it was on the back of a pickup truck, seats added, across fairly rough roads. This was not good with Lynn's travel sickness. I watched with growing apprehension, and we bounced along, and she got paler and paler. Miraculously, she didn't throw up, but needed a while to recover before we began the tour, led by a female Navajo guide. The canyon is open at the top (the definition of a slot canyon), and has narrow passageways, smooth sandstone walls and dramatic beams of sunlight that create a magical atmosphere.

The journey back to town was equally as bumpy and Lynn had had enough by then. Her stomach didn't really settle that evening and all she could manage for dinner was a salad. This caused much consternation to the waitress who couldn't understand that someone would choose to eat so little!

The next day we drove on to the Grand Canyon Village at South Rim. I had booked us a 'Historic Cabin' for our three-night stay. Historic in that it was built in the 1930s! The US is a young country. The cabin was compact, a bed sitting room and a bathroom, but was quite adequate for our needs. We had arrived in the afternoon so, having parked the car and unloaded our luggage, we walked to the canyon rim for the first time.

It was breathtaking! Think you know what the Grand Canyon is like? Not if you have only seen photographs or film. It is so much bigger than you ever imaging. One mile straight down from the rim to the river. The other thing you notice is the colour range. From deep purple to yellow, and every variation in between.

That afternoon we spent around the base, saving our excursions for the next two days. We walked up the the Bright Angel Trailhead and we drove further west to the visitor's centre for a different view. Then there was the helicopter flight. This was always going to be difficult for me, as I have already stated, I don't like flying. The thought of being in a small aircraft which didn't even have wings was close to terrifying and yet, this was the one chance we would have to see the canyon from above, completely unique. So, I booked our flight, but to be honest, I wasn't sure that I would board until I was climbing into the helicopter. Apparently, distributing the weight is important, and so we were all weighed before boarding and seating was allocated. This meant that I was in the back, while Lynn was sat up front with the pilot!

We took off, with commentary coming over the headphones we all had to wear. As we approached the rim, the commentary ceased, and as we crossed over, timed to perfection they played the theme from 'Superman'. You will believe a man can fly. All my fears evaporated, and the next twenty minutes was magical. Would I do it again? Probably not, but I'm glad I did it once.

On our last evening, we were on the east of the canyon and, as we looked along the canyon to the west, we could great bands of clouds rolling down the gorge. We retired to our cottage to spend the night eating junk food, sweets and snacks while I watched the Red Sox win the final game in the World Series breaking an 86-year losing sequence. I know almost nothing about baseball, but the emotion of the game was obvious to any sports fan, and I really enjoyed it. Lynn read a book!

Next morning, we opened our door to find that, during the night, three foot of snow had fallen! We walked to the rim and saw the amazing sight of the Grand Canyon covered in snow. If our first sight had been breathtaking, this was magical. Cold, but happy, we went into the restaurant for breakfast only to find that the snow had brought down some power lines and there was no hot food available. Except for biscuits and gravy! What kind of idiot eats biscuits and gravy for breakfast? Me. Still wondering why, it was awful, Lynn's muesli was much better.

Now I had the challenge of driving in these challenging conditions. We had a hotel booked in Sedona, where I had been planning a romantic end to our holiday. The plan was to go south on the AZ-64 and then turn off left towards Flagstaff and then Sedona. However, although the main roads were open, the smaller road that would have led to our destination was closed. Our romantic hotel was out of bound. I decided that we would turn right onto the I-40. To this point I had driven 60 miles in thick snow and needed a break. So, I stopped at the first place I found, The Pine Country Restaurant and Store, on Route 66. Refreshed, we carried on and, as we went further west, the weather cleared. By the time we got to Kingman, the sun was shining again, and I decided that this would be our overnight stay.

Realising that we now would have to stay in Las Vegas again before our flight home, I phoned the Orleans Hotel to book back in there. The receptionist was clear, this was the time of the International Bull Riding Finals, and all the rooms were booked, except for the Presidential Suite. I started to ring round other hotels, finally finding a room at the MGM Grand for our three extra nights. The cost was considerably more than the Orleans, but we had little choice.

The next day we drove to Vegas via the Hoover Dam and Lake Mead and booked into the MGM. If we thought that the Orleans was big, the MGM was enormous. It took over 30 minutes to walk from the entrance through the hotel to the swimming pools! The room was large and luxurious. That night we settled into our cloud of a bed and drifted off to sleep. Just around 2am, Lynn nudged me. "There's water coming through the ceiling". Drowsily I replied, "You're dreaming, go back to sleep.". She wasn't dreaming, water was coming through the ceiling next to the bathroom. I rang reception and they sent up maintenance who reported that there was a leak in the pipes between floors and it would take some time to fix. We were to be moved to a new room.

Sleepily, we got up, packed up our stuff and, helped by attentive staff, moved to another of the 6,852 rooms in the hotel. In our new room about 3am, Lynn immediately went back to sleep, but I was awake now, so I decided to go down for a hot chocolate. This is when I really began to understand the Vegas economy. It was the middle of the night, but the Casino was crammed with people busily losing money. I drank my hot chocolate amazed at humanity. Looking back, I realise that Las Vegas is a reasonably priced holiday, if you don't gamble. Gambling is what keeps Vegas going.

The next morning, we got a call to go to reception where we were offered an apology for the disruption in the night and an offer to dine that night for free in their best restaurant. My friend Ken, who had travelled in America with work, had given me advice. "Never accept a hotel's first offer". I had used this advice in booking the motels along our way and got reductions on a couple, but this was my big ask.

"Thank you,", I said, "but I don't think that is sufficient recompense for the middle of the night drama."

"What would you suggest?", said the receptionist. "Could you do something about the room rate?", I asked. A pause. "Would halving it be helpful?" Result! Our room rate was now the equivalent of the

Orleans! Together with a free dinner. Thank you, Ken.

We spent the next couple of days exploring more of the extravagance of the city, especially the fountain display in the evenings outside of the Bellagio, where the waters danced to different musical accompaniment. I loved Las Vegas, Lynn less so, but what an experience this holiday had been.

Again, we thought that this would be our last visit to the States, but we were wrong.

Five years later we were back again, in Orlando, with out great friend Mick and Janis Gibson. This time I didn't have the planning all my own way. Janis was a great organiser, and she knew some things that she wanted to do and so we compared ideas. Of course, Disney, Universal and NASA were on the agenda but there were a couple of additions, things that we hadn't done before. Jan wanted to go on an airboat trip at a delightful place called Boggy Creek which was noisy and fascinating. We also went to a wilderness area owned by Disney, but untouched. We walked through virgin Floridian landscape and ate our packed lunch by a lake as alligators floated past.

One evening stood out. I had discovered online a night club called 'Capones'. As the name suggest it was themed at a prohibition era speakeasy. All the staff were in character and there was a stage show which was very funny. The other big attraction was that it had an all you can eat buffet midway through the evening and unlimited drinks all night. We had a great night.

The other advantage of being with Jan and Mick was that they complemented us. Mick shared Lynn's problem of motion sickness, leaving Jan and I to experience all the rides while they entertained themselves.

The next year, we returned to America, but on the other side of the country. Dunstan had married his girlfriend from California, Caitlin Ferrara, in 2009. They had met at a friend's wedding in Los Angeles, and Caitlin had moved to the UK later, but her visa would expire in 2009, so they got married by themselves in Hawaii. This was very romantic, but they still wanted the big family wedding.

So, they planned a Marriage Celebration for 19th June 2010, in Santa Barbara, California, the place where Caitlin had studied at university. The best part of the whole thing was that Caitlin asked me to officiate the ceremony. I was delighted.

We didn't know who could make the trip of 8000 miles, but we began planning early. Christine and Jill and their families were the first to join us. We booked a house in Woodlands Hills, Los Angeles for six nights and then we would all move to Santa Barbara, staying for two nights which would include the ceremony. After that, we would split up, the Elliotts and Barrys going to Las Vegas and Lynn and I to San Francisco. Louise, Jon and little Jessica would meet us in LA for a day and then come to the ceremony in Santa Barbara.

The house was our ideal choice, but we had one letdown. The swimming pool, which was part of the deal, was out of order. Besides that, everything was fine, and we got ready for a few days of fun and adventure in LA.

On Saturday 12th June, we got to the house by different routes. Lou and Jon never made it to join us. Lou got hurt and couldn't travel, even though we tried to change her plans. This was a big disappointment and made Lynn sad for a few days, but we had to deal with it and move on.

We did our own things, since we had different interests, but we usually ate together at 'home' at night. The only exception was on Wednesday, when Dunstan and Caitlin took Lynn and me to their favourite Mexican restaurant, after a day of seeing the sights with them.

On Thursday night, we all went to Caitlin's parents' house for a 'Backyard Barbeque'. It was actually a much fancier event, with catering staff and a pianist to entertain us. David and Mary had prepared it. It was an unforgettable evening with great food and guests who were mostly family but also some neighbours. One of them was an old man who worked in the local radio and TV industry, like David. He had worked with some of the legends like Jack Benny and Burns and Allen, and we had a great chat about comedy and the differences between British and American styles.

The highlight of the evening belonged to Marty and Paul. When Caitlin first arrived in the UK, it was for Christmas 2007 when she stayed with us. It must have been a challenge to stay with people she didn't know and meet Dunstan's friends and family. On Boxing Day, we all went to Paul and Jill's house for the evening. Everybody who knows Marty and Paul know that no-one is safe from their teasing and, since Caitlin was the new girl, she got more than her share. But she coped more than well, telling us that back home she had three 'drunkles' who had inured her to this kind of behaviour.

Now, back to that evening in LA. The 'drunkles' were in attendance and halfway through the evening Marty and Paul disappeared, only to return wearing special T-shirts proclaiming the British Drunkles 2010 USA tour. Thereafter the party did degenerate into a British invasion evening, with us persuading the classical pianist to play show tunes for us to sing to and more. The bottom line was that a good time was had by all, and the Ferrara family now knew who we all were.

The day after that party, we all moved up the coast to Santa Barbara and the Ramada Hotel. That night most of us met together with David and Mary for an evening picnic on the beach. I could get used to the California lifestyle. The next day, 19th June, was the big day. Lynn and I started with breakfast at a seafront restaurant called Sambos, inappropriate but the food was excellent. As we strolled back along the seafront, I got a call on my mobile from my niece's boyfriend back in the UK. He said that Laura and my brother, Eddy, were in California and where was the wedding! Of course, they had been invited but we had no idea that they intended to come!

We spent the day relaxing before going to the venue for the celebration, where I had a rehearsal with the main participants. In the late afternoon we met on the hotel rooftop, under a hot sun to celebrate the wedding of Dunstan and Caitlin. I was impressed by how many Brits had come over to be with us. The service went well with the bride and groom choosing friends to speak. Dunstan had picked his friend Becky Jones-Owen who had persuaded other school friends to take part. Caitlin, for her part, had picked her friend, Noah Harpster, who gave the best wedding speech I have ever heard. No wonder that he became a Hollywood writer and actor afterwards.

The evening reception was fun, with another unexpected Kesseler guest. My nephew Danny arrived with two friends, after a holiday in Las Vegas. They had driven from there to be with us, made a mistake with the timing, missed the service, but arrived to enjoy the free bar! This day will always be a memorable moment in my life. How often do lay-preachers have the chance to preside over their son's wedding celebration? It was a privilege that I'm grateful to both of them for.

We had breakfast on the pier with the Elliotts and the Barrys in Santa Barbara on the 20th, and then parted ways. We went back to L.A. Airport to drop off the car and fly to San Francisco, where we got in the evening. I was feeling exhausted that night, maybe from the busy days before, so we ate at a self-service place and went to bed early. The next morning, I was still feeling unwell, so I rested while Lynn went to see the sights. She came back with theatre tickets for the musical, 'The Fantasticks'. This has the record for the longest 'off-Broadway' run and I had always wanted to see it.

It was only when we arrived in Santa Barbara that we found out that Dunstan and Caitlin had also planned to vacation in San Francisco. We didn't want to impose on them, but they arranged a dinner at a Chinese restaurant that Caitlin's mom had suggested on our second night. I was feeling better by then, and we did the usual San Francisco tourist activities for the rest of our time. We took a trolley car ride, went to the Golden Gate Bridge (it was foggy, we could only see the lower part), had food at Fisherman's Wharf and saw other local attractions.

On the 24th, we rented a car and continued to Monterey, staying in a very mediocre rental for four nights. The first attraction that I had arranged was the Aquarium on the famous Cannery Row. Lynn was sceptical that this would be worth it, but the Aquarium was amazing. Larger and more impressive than anything either of us had seen before, it also had a viewing platform overlooking the bay where sea otters could be spotted in the kelp.

We came to Monterey mainly for the Blues Festival. It was our first real music festival ever and, as of now, it's still the only one we've been to! It was outdoors, with three stages, and we enjoyed it a lot. The day started cloudy but improved later on. We saw different kinds of performers, from acoustic blues to loud blues, from traditional to modern. The food area was interesting, with stalls selling everything from grilled roadkill to deep fried Snicker bars.

The big surprise happened in the late morning, we were sitting and listening to a young harmonica player when someone tapped my shoulder. It was my brother Eddy, with his daughter Laura and son, George. I had mentioned our plans to them in Santa Barabara and they had not only remembered and bought tickets, but also spotted us in the crowd! We didn't stick together for the whole day, but we decided to meet for breakfast the next day. I got the impression that George enjoyed the breakfast far more than the Blues Festival!

We started our two-day journey back to LA the following day. The Big Sur drive was beautiful, as people had said. On the first day we took pictures at the Bixby Bridge, which was built in 1932 and is one of the highest single-span concrete bridges in the world, stretching 714 feet and standing 280 feet above the Bixby Creek gorge. We had lunch at a roadside restaurant that looked appealing, and it was. It had a small river behind it and tables in the water where customers ate their lunch and splashed their feet at the same time. We kept ours dry.

The petrol gauge kept dropping and Lynn grew more anxious as we drove. I also felt some worry until we reached a small town that had both a gas station and a motel where we could stay for the night. This was another motel with a view of the ocean and a very nice Italian restaurant for our second-last night in California.

We spent our last night at a Holiday Inn Express in Santa Monica, where we visited the famous pier that marks the end of the well-known Route 66 on our last day. When night fell, we drove to Las Angeles Airport and took the overnight flight back to England. The whole trip had been unforgettable, seeing places that Lynn and Blair as kids would have only watched in the 'movies'. If this was our final time in the States, it had been a great one.

It turned out that we had one more American adventure ahead of us. The next year we came back to our favourite place, Anna Maria Island, and stayed in a villa with Christine and Marty. As I have mentioned, Anna Maria is a relaxed, old-fashioned Floridian resort and we enjoyed a lovely, peaceful holiday. Some of the best moments were going back, for us, to Myakka State Park, dining on the beach and joining the start of Christmas in the Town Square, with fake snow.

We also spent a day, kayaking on Sarasota Bay. We didn't see any Manatees, but it was an unforgettable experience to slide through the mangrove swamps at the end of our day.

We had booked the villa for two weeks, but Marty and Chris had decided to take a few days in Orlando to visit Disney and Universal. At the last moment we decided to join them, for one night, and to take them for a visit to Capones, where we had last been with Janis and Mick. Chris and Marty had booked a car for themselves for this trip and so we travelled to Orlando separately, staying at the Holiday Inn Express. After a day at Universal, we took a taxi to Capones.

Our visit started off in a way that matched the rest of the night. We got there early and were told that we could go to the bar, but our free drinks would only start when we sat down at our table. Marty was the first to get to the bar and ordered a beer for himself and liquor for the rest of us. The barmaid, acting like a speakeasy barmaid, poured his draft beer and turned around to pour the spirits. Marty took a sip of his beer and, when the barmaid turned around, pointed at the glass and said, "Are you going to fill that?". She looked at him, grabbed the glass, filled it up and slammed it back on the counter with "Here you are, ya bum!". Everyone laughed. Until we got to our table and saw that she was our waitress for the whole night. She was great, liked our sense of humour and gave us drink after drink. At the end of the night, she gave us, not sold us, souvenir glasses. She did get a generous tip.

After we left the club with all that drink, Lynn, Christine and I were very drunk. I, wrongly sent our taxi away, thinking it was not ours, and we had to wait a long time for another. I had forgotten that our Thursday night outing had now become Black Friday morning and that taxis were busy taking customers to stores that opened right after midnight.

The next day, the Elliotts left to go swimming with dolphins, and Lynn and I chose to spend some time at Universal. We were amazed by what we saw when we got there. The park had been normal the day before (Thanksgiving), but after Thanksgiving, Christmas had begun. In one night, the whole park had changed into a winter wonderland, with Christmas trees and decorations and snow. They did it all while the park was shut to keep up the magic. I'm sure that this kind of display is something that Americans are very good at.

We enjoyed the rest of the holiday as much as the beginning and we departed, very satisfied. This time, this visit was our final one to the USA and with aging and insurance becoming more and more costly, I am fairly certain that it will be our last.

Although I despair of the politics sometimes, I love the USA and am so grateful to have got there as many times as we did.

CHAPTER 13 - ST BASILS – HEAD OF FUNDRAISING

As soon as she took charge, Jean started a comprehensive reorganisation of the company. She engaged every staff member, at all levels, and we all started to feel that we were truly a valued part of the organisation that employed us. Our ideas and opinions were heard and, as the changes were carried out most could see that they would be helpful in the long-term. Looking back, they were. For perhaps the first time in its history St Basils was made financially stable without losing the care of young people that had been its core since its inception.

Of course, for me, the big change was that I was now leading the fundraising team. Generally, this was well accepted by the current team. Michael, who had also applied for the post, was gracious in his acceptance and supported me well until his retirement. Suki Sahota was slightly different. Her work ethic never changed but I always felt that she compared me with David Goss and in that comparison, I came a poor second!

Perhaps this is the time for a brief mention of some people who served as members of the fundraising team under my management. Michael Norris was in charge of fundraising from Charitable Trusts. This suited his temperament. He was well organised and meticulous and very successful. He also went on to organise our walking challenges and to produce our charity theatre events, of which more later.

Suki Sahota was in post as fundraising secretary when I joined. She was efficient, committed and not afraid to speak her mind in team meetings. As I intimated above, I never felt that she was completely happy with my management style, though it never affected the effort she put into the job. She eventually left to take up the secretarial post in another charity. After she left her post was filled firstly by Bozena Starewska, a young woman of Polish descent who quickly became a valued part of the team and continued to volunteer for St Basils even after she had left employment.

When Bozena left the role was taken over by my friend Janis Gibson. I had known Janis for many years, and she had very successfully managed her own franchise with a cosmetic company in the past. She brought the best organisation to the department and, for me, almost acted as a PA. Although she had only come is as cover, she became integral to the organisation and her commitment to our events and the ethos of St Basils got her noticed by Senior Management. She was eventually 'poached' by Jean Templeton to become her PA, a post she held very successfully.

Steve Rainbow is a great character. He joined us as a Fundraising Officer, but his main joy in life was, and is, film making. He already had a portfolio of short films when I met him, and I was lucky enough to feature in another couple of his productions later. There will be more about Steven and films in another chapter. However, as a fundraiser, he became a long-term integral member of the team, eventually taking over the walk organisation from Micheal, and making it his own. He is still there, now in charge of all events.

Georgia Dent was not with us for a long time, but she certainly made an impression. Although she had no previous experience in charity work, she soon became engrossed. After she left us, she continued in her work for good causes and is presently the head of the Somerset Wildlife Trust.

Meredith Davison was, for a time, one of my 'buddies' in the team. I even helped to officiate at her wedding! A bubbly personality and open minded, she was one of the team members who reacted positively to the short reign of Clare Cassidy. When I took over, she continued to be a great support.

Rebecca Cheesman was an elegant young woman with one daughter when she joined the team. My remembrance of her was her determination to succeed, her willingness to learn and her honesty. Whilst she was with us, she took maternity leave with her second child, but, for personal reasons, decided to move out of the area. I missed her contributions greatly. She now runs her own Yoga business.

There were other who came and went, some good, some just marking time. The ones I have mentioned were part of any success that I might have had, and I am indebted to them.

There is one other to mention, although she has appeared before. I did not officially manage Cathy Clarke, but we did work in the same office, and she was part of the 'team'. Always forthright she managed the PR and Media for the whole organisation. She was there when I joined and, by and large, did a splendid job. I am sorry that there were those towards the end of my time who felt that her post was unnecessary, and she was 'retired'. I still feel bad about this.

If only achieved anything during my years as Head of Fundraising, it was because of the cooperation of all of the above team members. Everything we did, we did as a team, and so everything we achieved, we achieved as a team.

There are many things of which I'm proud during these years that I should mention. Firstly, the Sleepout. I mentioned in the previous chapter that one of my first decisions as Head of Department was to bring the Sleepout off the streets. We decided to hold it in our car park in Allcock Street, the feeling being that we could impose security on the site making it safer for all participants, especially the young. It quickly became clear that the car park would not be of sufficient size and so we approached the council to close Allcock Street for the evening allowing us to overflow onto the street and under the railway arch. Amazingly, they were very supportive and did this without charge.

Moving the event to the car park meant that we could also use the Heath Mill Lane premises, meaning that we could offer hot refreshments throughout the evening from the canteen, and use of the toilets (very important). We also decided to use the chapel for a midnight service, and we were thrilled when the Bishop of Birmingham agreed to officiate. We continue to operate this way the rest of my time in post, and Sleepout continued to grow during this time becoming a recognised part of the Birmingham calendar. Many times, the event was covered by local television and our midnight services were always full. The fact that it was warmer in the chapel them on the car park may have had something to do with this of course!

Whilst we paid for professional security, like every other event, the support of volunteers was essential. We had people patrolling throughout the night, volunteers providing hot food through to midnight and then breakfasts from 5:30 AM. The most incredible part was the genuine feeling of community with people feeling that they were actually making a difference by being there and coming year after year. I'm very proud that as I write this Sleepout continues to draw huge crowds in its new home at Millennium Point.

The other major fundraising event was "The Big Walk.". Following on from the Dartmoor Yomp, and the major difficulties we had with the weather on our second attempt, it was decided that from now on our walks would be circular, beginning and ending at the same point, and marshalled around the course. We would offer two challenges, one of about 25 miles and a shorter course of around 13 miles. We planned to have up to 6 checkpoints on the course, at which each team would be recorded, their ability to continue checked, and water and chocolate given out. The latter was made available by the generous sponsorship of Cadburys, which continued for many years until they were taken over.

This was the event that always stretched our organisational capability. Having made the decision that each year we would have a different course (to entice regulars back), Nick Venning had to find and trial a new route every 12 months. This also meant finding places where we could set up the checkpoints, getting agreement from landowners or local councils, and finding a headquarters to start and finish the route. This would often be a local school where we could use the car park.

The plan was that the first walkers would leave at 7 AM and so our staff and volunteers had to be there the night before to set up and early on the morning to be ready for the first arrivals. With the sponsorship from Cadburys, we were able to put all of our volunteers into a local hotel for two nights. On the night before the event, we would gather for dinner and the briefing for the following day. On the day itself every team would be checked in and every team member given an armband. This would be removed when they checked in at the end of the walk so that we knew who was still out on the course.

The first checkpoint would also be where team photographs would be taken, and these would be printed onto the certificates that every Walker would receive after completion.

I cannot emphasise enough how important the team of volunteers were for this event. They had to be reliable, flexible, responsible and enthusiastic. Over the years we built a core that became friends as well as colleagues and turned up year after year. For many years Michael Norris was in charge of organisation with the help of Nick Venning, whilst I would take responsibility on the weekend of the event itself.

Over the years, the walk took place all over the country. We visited the Lake District, Bakewell, the Brecon Beacons and many other venues. Each walk brought its own challenges of organisation and stories from the people who took part. One walk in the Peak District introduced us to a team who call themselves "Mitra Milan". They were all of Asian backgrounds and completely ill-equipped for the challenge that faced them. Many of the women were dressed in saris with footwear completely unsuitable for the muddy tracks and the men were not much better! Most of the team withdrew at the first checkpoint and we were certain that we would never see them again. We were wrong. Not only did they return the following year, better equipped, but they returned every year thereafter and formed a walking club that tackled challenges all over the world.

Many companies would use the event as a "teambuilding" exercise, and many came year after year. This added to the celebration feel on the day itself as people greeted each other at the beginning of the new challenge. By the end of my time the organisation became like a well-oiled machine from the reception in the morning to the meal for all the competitors at the end of their efforts.

Of course, with over 300 people competing there were risks to be managed. We partnered with St John's Ambulance to provide first aid and always have a vehicle available to pick up "casualties" from any checkpoint and bring them back to base for treatment. Whilst we had the normal blisters and twisted ankles, I'm glad to say that over the years that I was involved we only ever had one hospitalisation, and that was a member of the staff team who went down with sunstroke for lack of suitable headwear.

Again, as I write the "St Basils Walk" is still going strong having gone through many changes over the years. I am proud of the legacy of Sleepout and The Big Walk as I look back at my time as Head of Fundraising.

It is interesting to look back on the 'odd' ideas that actually made it to fruition. There was a television show, presented by a now discredited DJ, that offered to make viewers dreams come true. We decided to try and emulate it with our version 'Basil will Fix It'. The first request came from a Church of England vicar who wanted to be a maître d' for a day. So, we fixed it. With the aid if the St. Johns Hotel in Solihull, we organised a dinner which he 'took charge of', with the obvious help of the staff. We needed an entertainer and so I approached the Birmingham comedian, Don Maclean, famous for, among other things, presenting Crackerjack and having his own Sunday morning radio show on BBC Radio 2. Don agreed to entertain and was a great success. Thus began a great relationship between Don and St Basils.

Another supporter of ours was Norma, who wanted to produce a variety show! So, we booked the Alexandra Theatre I for a Sunday evening and she put together a show with local amateurs and celebrities. The celebs included Don Maclean and Prof. Carl Chinn.

We sold a lot of tickets and made a decent profit. The opening act was children from a local dancing school, always a good idea because their parents would buy tickets! However, in front of the Alex stage there is a deep orchestra pit, and, at rehearsal, it became fairly obvious that the 4-year-olds, dazzled by the lights, were in grave danger of dropping into oblivion. My task, therefore, was to patrol the pit, ready to catch any falling child. On the night, no child fell, which was a shame because it would have been great theatre!

This show prompted the idea of an annual show and Michael Norris was appointed to assemble the show. We did a number of shows at the Alexandra Theatre, and one at the Birmingham Hippodrome, which is a gigantic theatre and proved hard to fill. We booked and paid for a headline artist who we felt would bring in punters, but the rest of the cast would be professionals working free for charity. Don Maclean was in every show. Every time he was hilarious, and every time he refused any reimbursement of expenses. His attitude was simple, "If it's for charity, its free for charity". Sometimes he would bring his friend and fellow comic, Malcolm Stent and they would perform together and separately.

This began a friendship with Don, and we shared a few gigs together. I remember one in particular. It was an Accountants Ball, and we were the adopted charity. The after-dinner speakers were Don, Giles Brandreth and me. When we met in the green room before the meal Don pointed out that Giles had been allocated 20 minutes, he had been given 15 minutes and I was granted 2. He thought that over emphasised my importance! Don was never less than generous, always funny and a true Brummie.

2007 saw big changes in our family. Louise married her long-term boyfriend Jon Emmett in the beautiful parish church in Thame, Oxfordshire where they had settled. As father of the bride, I could not have been more proud of my lovely daughter on her big day. Our first granddaughter, Jessica, was born on 11th December that year and I had to leave the St Basils Christmas party to meet her at the hospital. This heralded the next phase of my life, a grandad!

As I approached my 65th birthday in August 2009 I had to consider retirement. To be honest, it was a prospect which frightened me. What would I do with my time? How will I cope financially? These and many other thoughts dominated as I contemplated my future. Lynn had already taken early retirement from the Blood Transfusion Service which was no longer the organisation that she had always enjoyed working for. She was in no doubt that we could manage financially and that I should retire.

There was no pressure from St Basils, but I began to realise that, although I could have stayed on, I felt I would be taking the salary under false pretences, as I had run out of ideas. I still had the passion for the organisation and the work that it did, but I felt that I could do more as an outside volunteer than as the paid Head of Fundraising. I decided that I would leave at the end of April 2010, the financial year end. I had a proud record of always hitting the fundraising targets and wanted to make sure that my last year lived up to the previous ones.

The day arrived with no warning of a 'send-off', although I was sure that there would be an in-house gathering. Sure enough, just before lunch, I was summoned to the meeting room where I fully expected to be greeted by my colleagues. Little did I know that much work had gone with Lynn and that not only were people from all over St. Basils, but many friends and family. It was unexpected and very moving. Jean made a very good speech, and I was presented with various gifts, including a 'This is your life' book with collected memories and photos from my life in and out of Fundraising.

In it Jean had written the following.

"Dear Blair,

It is with some personal sadness and considerable trepidation that I view your departure. I have come to rely on you to fulfil so many roles within the organisation, as we all have. You will leave not just one gap but a number, having funded our fancies, and some follies; married us; consoled us; persuaded us and even buried us!

Gravitas is a good word! It's one that you don't often get the chance to apply. It suits you well and we shall hugely miss the 'Gravitas' you bring to and for St Basils."

After the lunch, I returned to the Fundraising Office, cleared my desk, packed the car and drove home. Thus ended the most satisfying period of my working life and began another new adventure. Little did I know what was in store for me!

A week later, I wrote a 'Thank you' letter to Jean Templeton. I quote from it here.

"it is important that I thank you particularly for your contribution. The presentation that you did was terrific, even if my wife is still waiting to find out who it was about. She certainly did not recognise me from your nice words. Rev. Graham Spicer summed it up well when he reminded me that the next time somebody says so many good words about me, I'll be dead!

There is one more thing that I wanted to say on the day but decided against on the basis that it would probably embarrass both of us, but I do want to share it with you. In my fifty years of work, I have had many bosses – but you have been the best. You have challenged me and encouraged me, argued with me and listened to me, advised me and confided in me. It has been a pleasure to work with you."

It is strange in a way that I began and ended my career working for ex-patriot Scots. That, however, was the only similarity. Douglas J Moir could only see the faults in me, Jean managed to draw out some strengths.

CHAPTER 14 - ME AND THE BIG C

This account of my life would be incomplete without a chapter on one of the most life changing episodes.

I began to notice a problem with swallowing early in 2013, with food occasionally getting stuck in my throat. It became a nuisance in March, when we were on holiday in Rome and so I decided to tell my GP when next I saw her. To cut this story short, she sent me for tests at the Queen Elizabeth Hospital and in June I was diagnosed with Cancer of the Oesophagus. I decided to keep notes from that date and the rest of this chapter will consist of extracts from those notes and the 'Bulletins' I sent to friends and family during my treatment.

As far as I am able, I have kept the wording exactly as it was written in 2013, any explanatory notes are indicated in italics.

Sunday 16th June 2013

OK - so I am starting by cheating a little! I am actually writing this on Tuesday, 18th June having just installed this Journal/Diary app *(on my iPad)*. The idea is that I will be recording the happenings and my thoughts following my diagnosis with cancer (Which will really happen tomorrow!) However, I wanted to start with an entry for Sunday because it was the last day before the diagnosis. The last 'normal' day if you like. The truth is that I was somewhat anticipating the result of the tests so that even this day was coloured by those thoughts, but it was a good day and worth recording. I began it by leading worship at Rother Street URC in Stratford-upon-Avon. It was one of those services which went really well. I concentrated on the oneness that we all share in Jesus Of course; some things stand out. I felt a frisson when I spoke about those of us who have 'more days behind us than in front of us!' Back to Birmingham to pick Lynn up and then to Kingston Blount for a birthday barbecue for Tegan. It was a lovely afternoon with family. *(Kingston Blount is where Louise's in-laws live)*

Monday 17th June

The big day. Following my request the QE had given us an early 9:30 appointment. The meeting was between Lynn, me, the doctor and a MacMillan nurse. The diagnosis was that I have a malignant tumour in my oesophagus (gullet). It is about 5cm long and, with present information, probably operable. I am booked in for some minor surgery on Monday 24th, keyhole surgery on my stomach to see if it has spread to there. Pre-op will be on Friday, which means no holiday in Devon! Then more tests, a PET scan (aimed at spotting any secondaries) and a specialised endoscopy. These still have to arranged. Then probable chemotherapy and maybe surgery. Terrific support from both the doctor and the MacMillan nurse. Lynn and I went to Costa's and, over coffee and a scone, discussed how we were going to tackle it and immediate plans. Tell Lou and Dunstan first, tonight, and then the rest of the family tomorrow. We are not going to be shy about it. I'll continue with preaching appointments while I can and tackle things like the St Basils Concert and Anniversary service as soon as possible. My reaction is strangely muted. Helped, I guess, by the fact that I had suspected this for some little time. At this moment, not too scared and reasonably controlled. We carried on to Peg and Normans and took them off to the Town Hall for the Organ concert which they both enjoyed, as did I. Later in the evening I called both Lou and Dunstan with the news. Tried to be up-tempo and they took it as well as could be expected.

Tuesday 18th June

I had arranged to meet Lucy *(Hackett)* tomorrow (Wednesday) and I will let her know then but had sent Steve *(Rainbow)* an email saying I would talk to him tomorrow. However, he called me to tell me he would be away from tomorrow on leave. My hand somewhat forced, I gave him the news with a request not to spread it at St Basils, especially to make sure Janis only hears it from me! The idea behind this journal is to record my thoughts and experiences as the time goes by and more becomes known. I am going to try to be honest with myself. At the moment I don't feel too bad. A little worried about the future, of course, but no panic or overwhelming fear. The need is to get things properly organised, and that Lynn has all the information she needs to get on top of the bits of organisation that I presently do. I phoned Barbara and gave her the news. Not easy as she wasn't feeling too good herself. After lunch called the Barry's and Paul answered the phone. He was, as I expected, very supportive. Then called Christine on her mobile expecting her to be on the way home from her holidays but, unfortunately, she was at mother-in-laws. Making sure she was out of earshot I told her the situation. She was very upset, and Lynn then spoke to her. Next on my list was Keith Dennis. Good man that he is he offered to come round straight away but I dissuaded him. He will take over the organisation of the concert for St Basils. Peter Bates next, told him that I wouldn't be able to commit to anything for the foreseeable future. Colin rang and was sympathetic. Will ring Val tomorrow. Evening spent enjoying ourselves! Dinner at Cafe Rouge, followed by a brilliant concert at Symphony Hall by Hugh Laurie and the Copper Bottom Band. Busy day, but much got through. Lynn will tell her morn tomorrow and I will catch up with some others. Honestly, it is a strain but has to be done and the sooner the better.

(Notes on names. Lucy Hackett and Steve Rainbow are both members of the Fundraising Team at St Basils. Janis is Janis Gibson, close friend and, at this time, working at St Basils. Barbara is my sister. Paul Barry is married to Jill, my sister-in-law. At this time Paul has already been diagnosed with an incurable cancer. He was very supportive during my treatment. Keith Dennis is a good friend from church and Rev. Peter Bates was our Methodist minister at this time, Colin [McIlwaine] was our Moravian minister. Val [Dickens] is also a church friend)

Wednesday 19th June

Lynn went off to Yoga and I picked Lucy up from Brandwood and gave her a lift back to St Basils. This gave me the opportunity to tell her what was happening and how it may impact on the plans for the September service. The outcome is that we are going to move on quickly and get things organised before I start treatment. Also in the office were Ann and Ellie so they now know. I went across the courtyard and saw Janis and later Jean. Both sympathetic, of course. Called in at Tesco's on the way home and bought some lamb for dinner, which I cooked. Lynn, meanwhile, had gone over to her morns and told her the bad news. We've invited the Barrys and the Elliotts over on Saturday evening for a takeaway and a drink. Looking forward to that.

More names: Ann and Ellie were also in Fundraising at St. Basils. Jean [Templeton] is CEO there.)

Thursday 20th June

PET Scan. Back to the QE this afternoon for a PET scan where they inject you with a radioactive dye, make you lie still for an hour and then take another thirty minutes scanning your insides. You are allowed to take in your own choice of music, so I took the Easy Jazz collection. Good choice. We were the last customers for the day and left about 6:30.

Friday 21st June

Pre-Op Screening day. The QE appointments are/coming thick and fast! Today was a 12:45 appointment for my pre- op. First blood pressure (surprisingly good) and urine. Then a long session with a nurse going through medical history and present condition. She also gave us a good idea of what to expect on Tuesday and told me I must bring my CPAP and medicines in with me. After that I saw another nurse for swabs for MRSA, blood samples (4) and ECG. Lastly was examined by a doctor to make sure I was OK for the op. All seems well enough, so 7:30am Tuesday it is. I am nervous about Tuesday but will try and put off thinking about it until Monday. Here comes the weekend!

Sunday 23rd June

Toast for breakfast and then to church. Good wishes from Barbara Dennis and Brian Dickens During coffee Linda Ramdharry asked me how I was so I had to tell her. Like everybody else she was most supportive. In the afternoon Lynn rang Linda Beck and gave her the news and, in the evening, I called David Howarth to tell him and make arrangements for Ockbrook service in July. Also spoke to Sue Morris in the afternoon who has passed the news to the LibDem councillors and then, just before bed when I checked my mobile, I found that Ernie Hendricks had called round while we were at church to sympathise. People are kind. For me, I am feeling a growing apprehension about Tuesday, but nothing I think I can't handle. Unknown waters ahead!

More names: Rev. David Howarth is a Moravian minister, Sue Morris is a great friend and secretary to the Liberal Democrat Group on Birmingham City Council, of which Erbie Hendricks is a member.

Tuesday 25th June

Laparoscopy day. Writing this sitting in the waiting room in Ambulatory Care at the QE at 7:08am having arrived early. Nervous as a small feline. Hospital is weirdly quiet at this time of day and all the other patients waiting are, like me, silent. Feels like a church on Good Friday!

9:30 and I'm sitting in a hospital gown and my dressing gown waiting for my turn in theatre. I've been told that I'm no.2 on the list, but I've no idea how long a wait that entails. Been reading Elisabeth Sladen's autobiography but finding it difficult to concentrate. Might try listening to some music. Finally led up to theatre waiting at about 10am but then kept waiting for about 40 minutes before wheeled into theatre. Scared, but coped. Came out of the anaesthetic with a nurse at my side but she came and went before I was wheeled back to ambulatory care. Poor Lynn had had to wait well over three hours before she was called back in. I was in some pain, and more discomfort. Glad to drink water but when brought a sandwich I found that almost impossible to eat. I seemed to have no saliva. Pain relief was at last provided and, after checks, I was discharged just after 4pm. Lynn called Jill and she drove over and took us home. Glad to be home but in some discomfort. Jill decided that the paracetamol that I was sent home with wasn't enough and brought me some Co-codamol. Lynn went out and brought back sausage and mash for tea. Eating wasn't easy but I managed. Bed around 10:45 wasn't easy either but I eventually got comfortable and drifted off.

Friday 28th June

Second endoscopy. Didn't sleep well, coughing fit in the middle of the night. Got up early, had a black coffee (all that I was allowed). Took the bus to the QE and went in, very nervously for my endoscopy with ultrasound but was treated by a very understanding doctor. I think the level of sedation was less than the last time because I remember much more. Can't say it was pleasant, but I got through it. Had to wait afterwards to see the doctor who told me that they had not found anything else this time, which is good. Because of the delay by the time, I got back to Lynn the sedation had worn off and I was feeling quite good, so we had lunch in the QE restaurant, fish and chips for me. Travelled back on the bus to save money.

Friday 5th July

New QE appointment. Fairly uneventful day except that the hospital rang with a new appointment for Monday at noon. We anticipate that this will be when we get the full prognosis and treatment plan. If we get some notice of the treatment, we will try and take a holiday from Tuesday onwards. Tesco day today but I got a touch of melancholy while we were shopping. Just sort of drifted into it. Bought a couple of sponge puddings and felt a bit better! Lynn was very good. Invited to the Barry's for a barbecue tomorrow with the Elliott's. Part watched Murray win through to the Wimbledon final (too nervous to watch it all!). Lynn cooked fish for dinner and it was very good. Feeling much more cheerful by bedtime.

Monday 8th July

Prognosis. Slept very badly, could have been stress or just the heat! On the way to the hospital, we called at the doctors to collect my prescriptions and the at Next to buy more pants. Then on to the QE. Saw Sonya again and the news is good. The cancer doesn't appear to have spread and is, therefore, operable. So, I will be set up for 9 week of chemotherapy, followed by six weeks off before a major operation. The op will remove nearly all the oesophagus, connecting what is left directly to the stomach which is pushed up into the chest. Not exactly something to look forward to but, nevertheless, a good prognosis in the present circumstance. Returned home in good humour and immediately booked a caravan holiday for a week beginning tomorrow! Phoned everybody we could think of with the update, and I emailed my church friends with the news.

Name: Sonya Puig is my consultant surgeon.

Friday, 19th July

Cancer Unit Visit. Early 9am appointment at the Oncology Unit and we were well early. I have been offered the opportunity to be part of a Trial of a new Chemotherapy. Basically, it is the standard two drip plus tablets plus another drip if I am selected for the trial. As with everything so far, all the possible side effects are gone through in frightening detail. They want further lung tests and heart tests before we start, so it looks like three weeks before we start treatment. Then it is nine weeks of Chemo, followed by six to eight weeks to get the chemicals out of the system. Then surgery, then recovery, then a further nine weeks of Chemo. My best guess for surgery is December. March/April before the end of Chemo. Therefore, all being well, July 2014 before we can think of a holiday.

Tuesday 23rd July

Disappointment! Started the day by packing for my couple of days away and then off to the doctor's surgery for my asthma review with Nurse Anne. She was great, looked at my notes onscreen and said," This is the least of your worries right now then?" Dawn called from the hospital while I was with the nurse and so I called her back when I got home. The disappointing news is that she couldn't avoid Wednesday for my heart tests and so I won't be able to go for my art course after all. The good news is that there is now a timetable. Wednesday heart tests, Thursday lung function, Friday two appointments and then Chemotherapy should begin at 8:30 on

August 5th. Phoned and cancelled the course and the hotel.

Friday 26th July

More tests and a schedule. Ward 621 was my destination this morning for a new patient assessment. Another lovely nurse called Carmen this time, who talked me through all of the drugs involved in the Chemotherapy and their possible side effects. She showed my round the ward and it appears that you sit in reclining armchairs for your therapy. They give you a £4 voucher towards lunch (I wonder if I will want to eat?) and a free car park ticket. Appointments made; we went off to meet Donna in the Cancer Unit. She too is a very encouraging lady and, after a doctor had got me to sign consent forms for the trial and examined me again, Donna took over with the rest of the arrangements. I was given yet another sheaf of papers an sent off for blood tests and urine tests. Then back to the new hospital for lunch and an ECG. Interestingly, one of the forms I had to fill out was a Quality-of-Life questionnaire and this made me realise that I don't seem to worry about my condition as much as I thought I would. Wonder if that will change once I get started on Chemo on August 5th?

Monday 29th July

Worst day so far. I wasn't looking forward to today because I had got an appointment with the dentist, but I wasn't to know how it would develop. The dentist confirmed that I needed not one, but two, fillings but she was unable to do them straightaway because she had ricked her neck! A new appointment for tomorrow. Returned home to a message to ring Donna at the QE. The news was not good. The recent blood tests show that I am anaemic, too anaemic to go on the trial with a Hb of 8. So that was the end of my hopes of doing something useful with this embuggerance. Worse, it means that, at present levels, I can't start the normal chemotherapy. So, back to the QE for a blood sample for cross matching. Then on Thursday I go into ward 621 for two units of blood. I quickly descended into a black dog depression. Depression is a strange thing; you know you are depressed but can't seem to find a logical way out. The feeling lasted well into the evening gradually fading into the background over a takeaway Chinese. I now face the challenge of building myself back up before the treatment. Having hoped for a relatively quiet week, here I am with another full diary. Have to go back for more blood tests on Friday, so now we will go to the hospital early Friday and then drive down to Thame to see the girls. *(The girls being granddaughters Jessica and Tegan)*

Thursday 1st August

Transfusion day. Up early and off on the now familiar journey to the QE. The transfusion itself seemed to go well and we were ready to leave before 2pm, earlier than expected. The procedure took place on Ward 621, so it gave me a chance to get used to the surroundings and the way the ward works. Lesson one: must remember to plug the pump back in when I go to the lavatory!

Monday 5th August

Chemo 1. Taxi was on time, and we arrived on the ward by 8:30. However, not seen until 10 giving my nerves time to build up! When we did start, I was looked after by Mel, ward sister. Chemo hadn't yet arrived so I was started on a saline drip which would take a couple of hours. Easy start to what I expect to be more challenging as the day goes on. This entry being written at 11:18. Later. after chemo. Everything went as well as I could have hoped. No adverse reactions and actually not challenging at all. It turns out that there are three of us with cancer of the gullet. Tony is a man of my age who has had the op and is now on his last but one chemo. So, encouraging for me and Hassan who is really worried. Finished at about 4:30 and Jill came and picked us up. The evening was quietly spent and with very little side effects. Sent out a round robin bulletin to all those people that had sent messages of support.

Sunday 11th August

Even more tired. Today I was even more lethargic than before. Lynn went to church, and I tried to do some computing, but I really was too tired. So, I went and lay in the living room and listened to the radio. When Lynn came back, we had a sandwich lunch, but I still hadn't the energy to do much. Watched the Community Shield where Manchester United beat Wigan 2-0. Then watched the athletics from Russia. Lovely roast chicken dinner. The laziest day I can ever remember! However, still don't feel too bad. A little tinnitus has started today but nothing bad in the way of side effects.

Sunday 18th August

Church. Decided to go to church today. Lynn went first taking the newsletter and I followed five minutes before the service started. The service was led by a young lay preacher who was very enthusiastic but a little awry with some of his opinions! Great to see people all who continue to be very supportive. The bad news is that, Jane. the wheelchair user who sits in front of us, is in hospital for an operation to remove much of her liver, through cancer. I was able to give a little comfort to her morn, hope it helped a little.

Monday 19th August

Happy Birthday little Miss Kesseler. This morning, we went for a trip out to Baddesley Clinton, a NT place with a moat and lovely gardens. While we are looking at the scarecrows Lynn's phone rang, and it was Dunstan announcing the arrival of his baby daughter. Born just after 10 am and weighing in at 8lb 14oz but still with no name. Mother and baby well. Celebrated with shepherd's pie in the tearoom, before we came home. Stopped on the way home to buy some Prosecco for celebration later. Did get tired today but am considering driving to London on Wednesday to see new granddaughter. Maybe stay in the Travelodge on the way back. See how it goes.

Tuesday 20th August

Change of plan Having taken advice from Paul, I'm not going to drive down to London. Thinking about it made me realise that it was probably a challenge too far at this time. I spent the morning completing some artwork and after lunch Lynn went to Pegs armed with photos. While she was gone Dunstan called me to say that everyone was well, but Caitlin was having some difficulty in breast feeding so they were still at the hospital. Maybe released late today or tomorrow. I then had the great pleasure of talking to the new mum herself. She seems fine, apart from that one little worry. We had a great chat and it really cheered me up. Another day when I have felt quite well. Tired as before but coping. Of course, we begin again next week!

At this point, I was being overwhelmed with good wishes, cards and messages. Unable to contact everybody individually, I decided to put together a 'Bulletin' when went out on email. The text of it follows.

First Bulletin – 20th August

Dear friends, family and supporters,

First of all, thanks again for all of your continuing support. The "get well" cards. I have received now almost cover the door of my office at home. Couple that with the phone calls, text messages and emails and I feel quite overwhelmed at people's concern for my well-being!

The truth is, 2 weeks into my first chemotherapy sessions, I am feeling pretty good! I have been lucky enough not to have any of the major side-effects from the treatment so far. In fact, the only 2 real problems I have are tinnitus and ongoing tiredness, both recognised side-effects. So, all in all, I feel a bit of a fraud!

A number of you have asked for a little more detail of what the therapy entails and for the timetable from now on. If you're not interested in this scroll down to the headline "Good News".

The type of chemotherapy that I am receiving is known as ECX chemotherapy, where the E is for epirubicin, the C is for cisplatin and the X for Xeloda. On my first chemotherapy session at the Queen Elizabeth hospital. Cisplatin was the first drug given as an infusion over about 4 hours. Interspersed with saline, the second drug was the epirubicin, which is given as a 20-minute injection by a nurse. This is also a very bright red and, as another patient told me, turned your urine from a dark sauterne to a delicate rose within 10 minutes!

The Xeloda is taken over the next 3 weeks in tablet form, 8 tablets per day. On top of this I am, of course, taking my normal range of tablets for my multitude of minor ailments.

As far as we know at the moment the future looks like this; I'm seeing my specialist this Friday (23rd) and will be having blood tests on Monday (26th). My second chemotherapy session is on Tuesday the 27th and, hopefully, my third and final session will be on Monday, 16th September. So, my chemo will be finished by 7th October. Then 6 to 8 weeks later the operation. This will be followed by another 3 sessions of chemotherapy.

"Good News" Yesterday, the 19th of August, Lynn and I became grandparents for the 3rd time! Dunstan and Caitlin became proud parents of a little girl at 10:10 AM with a birthweight of 8 lbs 14 oz. Mother, baby and slightly frazzled father all doing well.

Friday 23rd August

Consultation and Birthday. 11am appointment at Cancer Clinic went OK, although we managed to get lost on the way from the new QE to the old! One concern was that I might need another transfusion, but after blood test it was decided that I was alright. In the evening, we went to Aalto to celebrate my birthday. Lovely meal, I had a scallop and pork belly starter, followed by Monkfish in a mussel chowder. Sweet was a champagne jelly with fresh raspberries and a strawberry granita, all washed down with a bottle of Prosecco. Travelled in on the bus but home by taxi. A good day. Lots of birthday cards and good wishes on Facebook. Feeling good as in the past days. Still tired, even though I am at the end of a chemo cycle.

Monday 26th August

Lynn to London me to QE. Lynn did feel good enough to go to London, so I went to the QE for my blood tests on my own arriving there about 9:30am. Because it was Bank Holiday the place was deserted, very strange. No problem with the tests, back tomorrow for chemo. Lynn had a good day in London with the family. Caitlin a bit up and down, crying when Cora is distressed. However, Lynn says that they are generally coping, and Dunstan is doing well. Lynn continuing to sleep in spare bedroom as she has now developed cold sores and doesn't want to risk passing any infection to me.

Wednesday 28th August

Mixed day. Slept very badly last night. I had forgotten that I was the same first time, but when morning came, I was still very tired and feeling quite weak. The morning was a struggle and after lunch I went back to bed and slept until 4. When I got up, feeling much better, Peter Bates was here talking to Lynn, so he stayed on for coffee and a chat and was joined about 4:30 by Micky Gibson on his way home from work. Two very welcome visitors. Call from Louise on holiday in Rhyl. They have had a good day at the fair and at the beach and she has spoken to Dunstan who reports that his family have had a good day too. I felt much better after the rest but did notice some slight nausea before bedtime. Took the tablet and some Gaviscon before lights out. Still sleeping alone because of Lynn.

Thursday 29th August

Feeling icky today. Slept reasonably well, waking about 4am and having difficulty getting back to sleep, but then sleeping on and off until Lynn came in at 9. Felt okay, but a bit nauseous and not feeling like eating. Had some cereal to cover the pill taking but the feeling of nausea got worse after I had washed and dressed so I took to my bed about 10:30 and stayed there until 1 pm. Feeling much better, but not anything close to right. Lynn, who was very supportive, suggested porridge for lunch and that went down quite well. I am writing this at 3:10pm and Lynn has gone off to Sainsbury for some shopping. It seems to me that my reaction to the chemo is somewhat worse than the first time. Maybe this is to be expected as the poisons build up in my body. We'll see. Carrying on this diary entry at 10:30pm. Continued to feel nauseous throughout the day and really did not feel like taking my pills this evening. However, Lynn cooked a lovely, tasty stir fry which tempted me to eat, and I did feel a little better thereafter. Hoping I will sleep better tonight. Lynn is warning that I may continue to feel poorly tomorrow. I'm just going to have learn to live with a tougher challenge.

Monday 2nd September

Worst day so far. Really feeling quite wretched today. Tinnitus is certainly worse, and belly is upset. No energy level goes without saying. Also spoke at length to Nick Venning who has received my PowerPoint presentation and will look through it. It is strange how the sixth day has been the worst both times (at least I hope it's the worst!) by the evening I was beginning to feel a little better, then I suddenly go the 'flashing lights' migraine warning, so I went to bed about 10pm. Lynn woke me up at midnight for my pills, but I dropped off again. *(The PowerPoint presentation was for the St Basils 40th Service. Nick was standing by in case I was unable to take part)*

Sunday 8th September

Church today. Lynn left for church early because she was on coffee duties. I followed and arrived with 10 minutes to spare. Arrived at the same time as the McIntosh family. Ashton has recovered somewhat from a hospital stay following a fall caused by his Blood sugar count dropping to 1! Lots of support for me but especially touching was the concern from Gwen Wells whose husband has the same condition as me, but inoperable. Even with her own problems she has time for others. Church attendance low because over 30 had gone to Llandudno for the weekend. Shame that it coincided with Anniversary Sunday. Colin and Peter shared the service with Peter preaching very powerfully on who owns the church. Took to my bed in the afternoon for a couple of hours and then got things ready for tomorrow. Dinner was roast pork with roast vegetables. Very good. I guess that I am now at my best in this cycle. This busy week will be a test, but one I'm looking forward too, especially Thursday.

Wednesday 11th September

Early starters. I have been keeping a record of my BP for a few days now with my new toy, but this morning I had to go to the GPs to see the nurse for a BP check. Turned out fine, which was interesting. Home for more work on Thursday's service. In the evening, we went to the newly reopened Rep to see a new Alan Bennett play 'People'. Great night out. This week is being a good one. I'm feeling good and we are getting out and about. I reckon that if the future is uncertain, it must be right to get the most out of the present.

Thursday 12th September

What a day! Morning spent getting everything together for tonight's service. Then, after lunch, to the QE for my first meeting of the support group. Tony was there to meet me, and we had a fascinating presentation about anaesthesia from a consultant. Learned a lot. Good to see so many patients and ex-patients looking so well and being so encouraging. Then off to St Martins to prepare. All went well except that Vicki was delayed and I had to start a bit late, and I had to bring the choir forward. But it all worked perfectly. I felt in good form. Vicki was great, Jean spoke very well, and Bishop David was superb. Good attendance with some notables like the Edmonds, Paul Tilsley, Jim Whorwood. Special for me was Anne Clarke, who came both for the service but also to see me. Cathy Clarke was there, and I upset her by telling her about my condition. Hard, but I don't want to hide it away especially as so many people know already. Left the church about 7:30, later than expected, tired but pleased at the evening. Fish and chips for supper and then watched the first episode of 'Peaky Blinders' on BBC. Bed at 11. However, I'm writing his at 2am having had to get up with terrible leg cramps which refused to go away. Crying with the pain, which woke Lynn, so I got up and walked about a bit and made myself a cuppa. I'll go back to bed a little later.

Names not previously mentioned. Vicki (Roberts) was a previous service user at St Basils, now an employee who helped me present this 40th Anniversary Service for St. Basils. Bishop David was the Bishop of Birmingham; the Edmonds were St Basil benefactors and Paul Tilsley and Jim Whorwood were both Liberal Democrats and past Lord Mayors. Anne Clarke is my cousin who lives in Plymouth, her sister, Jean, is the widow of Les Milner, the founder of St. Basils.

Friday 13th September

Payback day So tired today. But feeling good about yesterday, lovely emails from Jean and Lucy. Hospital in the morning at the Cancer Clinic, but for the first time in my experience they were running really late. At 11, my appointment time, a nurse came and apologised that they were an hour behind. Lynn was going to London to see Cora and couldn't really wait. So, she went off and I waited on my own. Good job because it was after 1 pm when I finally got out. Went home and had some lunch and crashed out. In the evening, I cooked the frozen pie in stock with a baked potato and baked beans. Good. Picked Lynn up from Solihull station at 10:30 and then earlyish bed. *(Cora was the name that Dunstan and Caitlin decided on for their daughter)*

Monday 16th September

Third chemo session begins. For some reason I felt really anxious this morning. Good job I have Lynn to jolly me along. The session itself was okay. No sign of Hassan though, I hope he's alright. Drove to and from the QE myself and that went well too. Home about 5:30. As the evening went on, I felt more unwell and, as before, found it hard to get to sleep.

Friday 20th September

Not yet getting better Still not good I'm afraid. As the day went on, I kept hoping it would get better, but it didn't. Ah well. Feeling quite down and realised that I am absolutely fed up with taking pills. It's really becoming an effort. Common sense tells me I have got to keep going and, of course, I will.

Saturday 21st September

Crap! Still crap. Just running on empty this time. No energy at all and feeling uncomfortable all of the time. Encouraged by watching Villa beat Norwich 1-0 at Carrow Road.

Sunday 22nd September

Not good enough for church, again This seems to be a worse session than before. Tired, nauseous, and plain fed up. Lynn went to Harvest Festival while I stayed home and did nothing.

Second Bulletin – 1st October

'Oh, I would be in the West Country', and so we were. We are just back from the heart of rural Cornwall where Lynn and I spent a week in a beautiful, converted barn on a farm between Redruth and

Portreave. The weather was kind, and we are celebrating the end of my chemotherapy.

As before, thank you all for the ongoing support that you give me and Lynn. To say it is appreciated is to understate the case. It really strengthens us. This month we have certainly needed it. For some reason the chemo seemed more aggressive this time round and I found it hard to do anything and hard to concentrate when I did attempt to do something. The tiredness and energy deficit are really draining, and I feel sorry for those who couple that with the more radical side effects that I have avoided. Still, I have only mild nausea and annoying tinnitus. Nothing compared to some of the people I have met in Ward 621 at the QE.

However, I took my last tablets last Monday. As I write this my stomach feels better than it has for weeks, and I am hoping that I will see some return of vigour. Not that I have ever been noted for my vigour!

I now am waiting for an appointment with the surgery team, which I expect will be in the next week or so. Then, hopefully, we will get some idea of a date for my operation.

In the meantime, life goes on. On 12th September I was fit and well enough to lead the Service at St Martin in the Bullring to celebrate 40 years of St Basils, the charity that I worked at for 16 years. The service went well, as those of you who were there know. The biggest thrill for me was my cousin Anne coming all the way from Plymouth. The Bishop of Birmingham (Bishop David) preached for us, the Bishop of Aston (Bishop Andrew) led prayers and with Bishop Peter Hall in the congregation there was more purple than you get in an Evesham plum harvest. My especial thanks go to my successor as Head of Fundraising, Lucy Hackett, who was kind enough to take a back seat for this event and let me and my ego take centre stage. The ego and adrenalin seemed to get me through, but it took three days to recover!

The next notable date in my non-medical diary is November 9th, when I am due to present a fundraising concert on behalf of St

Basils, organised by my good friend Keith Dennis. Entitled 'The Great American Songbook' and featuring the singer Marty Elliott, it will be at Hall Green Methodist Church beginning at 7:30pm. Tickets available for only £5 each and can be reserved via email to me. (End of commercial).

Since so many of you seem to want to know how things are going, I will produce another one of these when I know future operation dates etc. in the meantime, thanks again for the support. Oh, and here's the latest photo of my 7 weeks old granddaughter, Cora.

In October my brother Jon's lovely wife, Margaret, was very ill. The following entries mention her, Jon and their son, Danny.

Wednesday 16th October

Margaret - no improvement. I am feeling pretty good personally and it seems almost hypocritical of me to consider myself when others are so poorly. The latest news about Mags is that she now has contracted pneumonia and the end, it seems, is closer. Spoke to Danny who seems to be coping at the moment. I spoke to the QE, and they confirmed my appointment for this Friday at 10:00am.

Friday 18th October

Hospital. Appointment was for 10:00am. Saw Dr Kunene just after that. She was accompanied by Hazel, the Macmillan nurse, an ominous sign. It appears that the CT scan has found two items on my lungs. They could be cancerous secondaries, benign, who knows what, or the results of infection. The prognosis is powerful antibiotics for a week followed by a biopsy taken with local anaesthetic under the CT scanner on 7th November. The other news is that there is now a projected date for the op, November 19th. That could change with the results of the biopsy. Felt pretty low, Lynn was a great support. The strange thing was that I somehow expected the bad news since I had a 'feeling' yesterday. Brother Ed came round late afternoon. Teresa, his ex-wife is to have a kidney transplant from her mother. Mags is still with us but fading according to Barbara. What a family!

Saturday 19th October

Farewell to Mags Phone call during the night from Jon to tell us that Margaret died about 2:30am. Very sad. It's hard to believe that her vibrancy has gone from the world. Our thoughts and prayers are with Jon, Danny and the family of Mags.

Wednesday 23rd October

Richard II at the RSC. In the late afternoon we drove over to Stratford for pre-theatre dinner at the Opposition. I had a good steak. Then over the road to the Theatre and David Tennant as Richard II. He was superb but so was the entire company. My restricted vision seat was fine and, for £14, even better! Drove home feeling good, the afterglow that a good night in the theatre can give you. I have been a bit short tempered lately and, with the date for the op approaching, I'll probably get worse, but I must continue trying to hold it in check

Thursday 24th October

Flu jab day. Quiet morning, then off with Lynn to the surgery for our flu jabs. Nurse running very late, over 30 minutes. Asked her to check that there were no contraindications with my antibiotics, and she had to call the 'real' nurse in! However, there aren't, and we went ahead

Saturday 26th October

Jan and Mick. Evening visit from Jan and Mick bearing Chinese. Lovely evening chatting, sharing, remembering and hardly a mention of the big C. Good friends, as I have said before, are so important in our lives

Monday 28th October

Elliott's visit. Blood pressure very high this morning. Lynn makes the very good point that we have been eating Chinese for two whole days and it is very salty. Salt raises BP. QED. Updated Marty's web site in the morning but had to take a break with an incipient migraine. Finished it while Lynn went to buy biscuits for our afternoon guests. Chris and Marty arrived about one thirty and stayed a couple of hours. Good to see them. Barbara had rung me and asked me to place the death notice for Mags in the Mail. Problem was that their website just kept crashing. Eventually I found a phone number and they suggested emailing it to them they would set it and send it back for approval and payment. Sent the email but nothing came back before bedtime. Most annoying. Will call them in the morning.

Tuesday 29th October

Notice in Mail. Got notice placed in the Mail, eventually. Their system is rubbish.
Jon came round with some pictures of Maggie for the service sheet. Holding up.

Monday 4th November

Margaret's funeral. Met Louise at Solihull station and then went on to Corpus Christi where Dunstan arrived independently. Large congregation for the Funeral Mass which was very good. Father Michael was excellent and inclusive. My tribute which I expected to be part of the Mass actually took place in the Crematorium later. A large number came on to the cremation, filling the balcony and with many people standing. My piece did go down well. The wake was good. It is so encouraging to see Dunstan and Louise enjoying the company of their cousins, especially Jodie. We took Lou back to Moor Street and left Dunstan to find his way to New Street.

Wednesday 6th November

It takes a worried man.... Lynn spent the day looking after mother-in-law, who is a little better. I wrote up some notes for the show but found it hard to concentrate. My mind is on tomorrow and I'm not sure which I am more worried about, the procedure or the results.

Thursday 7th November

Another hospital day Up very early for the taxi to the QE for a 7:30 appointment at Ambulatory Care. Efficiently booked in but then had a long wait because they decided they wanted more blood samples. Eventually taken down to Imaging for the CT scan. It turned out to be clear and therefore no biopsy needed! Great weight lifted off my shoulders and we returned home triumphant on the 76 bus.

Friday 8th November

Rehearsal Feeling good today - I wonder why? Rehearsal for our show in the evening went generally well, worry about John Edmondson who is having real problems with his songs. Val is going to give him some extra rehearsal time

Saturday 9th November

The show. Down to the church at 6:30 to prepare. Disciples of Steel already rehearsing and sounding great. Marty arrives using Christine as his roadie! The audience starts to arrive very early and by the time I am ready for a run through there are about 30 people there. Decide to do run through with Marty but without microphone. Fingers crossed. People keep arriving. Surprised to see Eddie and Jon. Hazel brought Colin rather than Trudi. Jan and Mick and, of course, Sue and Alan. Quick count of the audience including performers about 140. Well pleased. Disciples of Steel got us off to a brilliant start. Colin's folk songs went down well and some of the audience sang along. Youth Club performed 'I am cow' to great amusement and then accompanied Peter Bates' Elvis routine. Dorries Ivor Novello song was also well received. My Professor Higgins got off to a sloppy start but got better and finished well. Johns' version of 'Softly as I leave you' was fine, the extra rehearsal worked well. The first half was finished in great style by the Harwood sisters singing 'Loathing' from 'Wicked'. They were simply brilliant. Marty was the best I've seen him with 45 minutes of songs and his communication with the audience was really good. Unusual for him to have a concert type audience but he handled it very well. Great response afterwards from an audience that had obviously enjoyed itself. Home in time to watch Villa win on Match of the Day

Sunday 10th November

Remembrance Sunday. More money came in before the service and we have raised an amazing £735 for St Basils. Considering that our target was £500 Keith, and I are well pleased. Colin handled Remembrance very well with a video link to the Cenotaph working really well. One of his better sermons too. Relaxing for the rest of the day. Feeling relatively relaxed and quietly confident.

UNRELIABLE MEMORIES

That marked the end of my diary entries with my surgery planned for 19th November. Immediately after the operation Lynn sent out an email to all my supporters (Third bulletin). There were two more 'Bulletins' and they are reprinted below.

Fourth bulletin

I know that Lynn has been doing a great job of keeping you all informed, but I've been home for over a week now and I really feel that I should take back the reins.

I'm settling back in at home to a completely new routine and everybody tells me that I am doing very well. I must confess, however, that I wish I was moving forward faster, but then patience has never been a Kesseler character trait!

As before, I have been overwhelmed by the cards and messages that you have been sending me. Whilst I was in hospital, Lynn would bring them in everyday and they really did make a difference, especially when things weren't going as well as they could have been. Thank you again.

One or two people have asked for more detail of my treatment and so this follows. However, if you don't want to read the (not too) gory details, you can stop reading here.

<u>The brief details.</u>

Of course, the truth is that I remember very little about the first couple of days. I remember being taken to theatre, the anaesthetist preparing me and then nothing until I woke up in ITU (Critical Care). Lynn tells me that the operation took longer than expected, around 9 hours, but the surgeon who came to speak to her immediately afterwards said that it had gone well. That was on the evening of Tuesday, 19th of November and I remember waking up the following day and talking to Lynn and Dunstan, who had come up from London. I felt pretty good, but that wasn't to last.

Surgeons had always realised that there may be a problem with my sleep apnoea. For the last 7 years, I have slept with a CPAP machine which provides a constant pressure of air to keep my airways open while I sleep. Without it, I wake up every 3 minutes or so as I stop breathing! The surgery team could not allow me to use the CPAP machine after my operation because of the extra pressure that it would bring to the join between what was left of my oesophagus and my newly reconstructed stomach. The last thing you want is to burst those stitches! So, they had come up with the idea of putting oxygen through a tube up my nose to compensate for the lack of the CPAP machine. It didn't work. That first night I was awake and fighting for breath until morning. Though the nursing staff were incredibly helpful there was no way I was going to sleep.

Next morning the surgical team had to put plan B into operation. I was to have a tracheotomy. Again, I don't remember any details until I woke up back in ITU with a tube in my throat and **unable to speak!** Those of you who know me well will realise that the next 6 days of silence were a huge test for me. But it did the job since I was now breathing through my throat below the place where my apnoea occurs, I could sleep. It was bliss.

The next few days were filled with building up my strength and learning to cope with the tracheotomy itself. Everyday brought a new challenge, usually from the physiotherapists, but everyday also brought a little more progress. Normally someone having my operation would have been out of ITU and onto a ward in about 7 days. For me it was 15 because they could not transfer me until the tracheotomy was removed.

At this point I have to pay tribute to the nursing staff in ITU. Since I was quite quickly one of the fittest patients in there, I was able to observe the amazing professionalism as they dealt with severely ill patients, with many different problems, with skill, humanity, care and an absolute commitment to maintaining the dignity of their patients. I can't speak too highly of them.

The final test for me before being sent to a ward was to be able to sleep for a night with my own CPAP machine. We manage this on the night of Monday, 2nd December and on Tuesday my tracheotomy was removed, and, in the evening, I was transferred to an ordinary ward. On Wednesday morning my surgeon announced that I was fit enough to go home the next day and, with the help of the staff on the ward I was prepared and able to come home on Thursday.

Now it's a case of building up my strength, learning to eat with my reduced size stomach. I'm still getting additional food supplement through a tube into my duodenum but I'm getting used to 6 small meals a day instead of the normal 3 large ones. It will take a long time to regain my fitness but most days I feel that I am moving forward.

During all this my major support has been, of course, Lynn. This time was made considerably harder for her because while I was in hospital her beloved mum died. Her funeral is tomorrow (Monday), and I would be grateful if all that support you have shown to me over the past few months could be directed to her for at least one day.

April 2014 – last bulletin

Dear friends, it has been some time since the last "Bulletin", but I have been waiting for this moment to bring you up to date.

Two weeks ago, I saw the oncologist at Queen Elizabeth hospital after finishing my chemotherapy course. I'm glad to report that they were happy enough to discharge me into the care of my surgeons. On Monday of this week, I saw my surgeon and she is pleased enough with my progress to say that she does not want to see me until November! Coupled with this she removed my feeding tube and I feel suddenly free!

The final round of chemotherapy was far, far worse than the one I had pre-operation. Whereas the first time round I had only minor side-effects this time round was much more testing. As well as the usual nausea and lethargy I managed to get dry peeling skin, bleeding mouth ulcers and sundry other nasties. My blood count also went down, and I had to have another blood transfusion. But all that is now behind me, and I can look forward to the future with confidence.

And this is the point where I have to say a huge "Thank You" to all of you for your support and concern. The last nine months has been, as they say on all the best reality shows, quite a journey. It is a journey that I would not have chosen to take, but since I had no choice, it has been a journey that has shown me the best in my friends, relatives and the professionals who have cared for me. I have been truly blessed.

Staff at the Queen Elizabeth Hospital have been, without exception, brilliant. From the moment that my surgeon placed her hand on mine as she confirmed the diagnosis to the pleasure that was obvious as she told me how pleased she was with me and that she didn't want to see me again until November. In between doctors, nurses, phlebotomists, receptionists, porters have all been terrific. Unfortunately, the NHS gets a lot of bad press-but when you really need it, it comes through.

However, the really humbling experience of the last nine months has been the support from you. The cards, the letters, the phone calls have all been positive and encouraging and at times truly moving. I will never be able to say thank you enough. It seemed that every time I felt a little bit low another card would pop through the letterbox and cheer me up. Please don't ever underestimate the amount of good that the simple things do.

These, coupled with the prayers of my Christian friends, have helped me stay optimistic and positive and I'm sure that these qualities help with healing.

This will be the last of these bulletins which I hope served to keep you informed in return for your support. The next thing for me and Lynn are holidays in Devon in May and then our big family holiday with Dunstan, Caitlin, Cora, Louise, Jon, Jessica and Tegan to celebrate my 70th birthday in August.

I write this as we approach the Christian festival of Easter, a time to celebrate new life. It feels very apt. May God bless you and all those you love in the days and years to come.

Thus ends my contemporary notes and looking back on them some ten years later has been instructive. For once these are Reliable Memories, written as the events happened. In the ten years that have followed I have realised just how lucky I have been. I was diagnosed early and was in the hands of dedicated, talented professionals thereafter. It is no exaggeration to say that they saved my life.

How did this affect me in the long-term? I have become more appreciative of life and the joys of friends and family. Physically, of course, there have been changes. Even there, I have been fortunate. For most people, post-op meals are taken smaller and more regularly, six small portions per day is normal, to accommodate the smaller stomach. I was one of the fortunate few that developed a stomach pouch, enabling me to go back to three meals a day and the weight gain involved!

Medication is, and will always be, ongoing. The main problem is that I have no valve at the junction of stomach and gullet, so stomach acid can flow backward into the throat, which is painful and damaging. The answers are acid reducing pills and learning to sleep sitting up! Minor inconveniences for ten bonus years of life.

POSTCRIPT – Me and the Big C, the sequel.

In early 2024, following a routine annual check-up, my GP sent me for a colonoscopy and a cancerous growth was found in my bowel. Tests and scans followed quickly and on May 13th, 2024 I was admitted to Solihull Hospital for surgery to remove part of my colon. As happened 10 years previously, the service that I got from the NHS was exemplary and, with a few minor hiccups, I was sent home 6 days later to recuperate. On Wednesday 26th June, I saw my surgeon who assured me that he had removed the tumour and that there were no further traces anywhere else. There will be follow-up tests at the end of the year.

CHAPTER 15 - GOODBYE TENSION – HELLO PENSION

Looking back, I realise that I was, initially, afraid of retirement. Afraid of being bored, of financial insecurity, of losing purpose.

To avoid boredom, I had started painting before retirement and, now having the time, started taking lessons. I found, and still find, great satisfaction in producing a painting or sketch. I work mainly in acrylic but have dabbled in pastels and pencils. One thing that my art teacher taught me that I have taken with me into other areas of my life, is that there is a time when you have to step away from a painting and say, "It is finished". It will not be perfect, but it is as good as it will be. I have found this to be just as true when writing sermons, producing church newsletters and cooking! Perfection is the realm of God, not man.

Financially, the credit goes to Lynn. She had retired a year earlier and had got her act together. She sat me down and persuaded me that, with her NHS pension and my bits and pieces of pension, we would be stable. Our mortgage was paid off, we had no major debts and we would still be able to go on the holidays I loved.

I took her at her word and within days of leaving St Basils, we were taking our car through the Channel Tunnel on our way to Bruges. We had a great time there, but our return was affected by the eruption of a volcano in Iceland. This spewed great clouds of dust into the air and aircrafts were unable to fly. Thousands were stranded, including Dunstan, who was in Madrid on business and couldn't get home.

We, of course, were not flying, but we were staying overnight in

Calais on the way home. Calais was full! Full of people trying to get on ferries and trains to get back to the UK. Luckily, we had pre-booked our accommodation, because all of the hotels were overcrowded. Dunstan, meanwhile, had to stay in Madrid. Not a bad place to be marooned and the local knowledge he acquired during his enforced stay became very useful to his Mom and Dad when we took a Madrid city break in 2016. Later in 2010 we returned to Anna Maria Island in Florida.

Bruges was just the start. Not being tied down to work patterns meant that we could take holidays out of season, whenever we pleased and had the money. Over the past fourteen years we have taken 53 holidays, an average of 3.8 per year! Cornwall was our most popular destination with 10 visits, boosted by the fact that for many years Lynn's sister Christine owned a caravan near Newquay where we got 'mate's rates'.

We were lucky enough to go to the Canary Islands five times and to Cyprus twice. Our only ever all-inclusive holiday in Menorca in 2014 pointed up a major change in me since my surgery in 2013. That brush with eternity has given me much more patience and Lynn was amazed that I could sit, happily by the pool reading instead of rushing all over the place. 2014 also saw me celebrating my 70th birthday, which I decided to do by taking my children and their families to Butlins at Minehead for a week. There was a mixed reaction to this with Caitlin non-plussed but granddaughters Jessican and Tegan enjoying all the 'free' attractions. Madrid in 2016 was memorable, but the best of all was the Rhine cruise that we took in the same year. Beginning in Cologne and finishing, eight days later in Basel in Switzerland. Everything about that holiday was at least as good as the brochure! Accommodation, food, excursions and the places visited were all special, especially because of some of the time we were retracing the journey made by Lynn's mom and dad some years before.

Retirement hasn't just been about holidays; it has given the time to be more active in the church. Without the encumbrance of employment, I have been able to take up more preaching appointments and got to Moravian Synod as a representative of our congregation. The biggest change, however, was that we closed on church and began another.

By 2007 our church in Sparkhill was, literally, beginning to crumble. Water leaks from above and a rising water table flooding the cellar were beginning to make the continuing use of the building as it was untenable. The Church Meeting made a momentous decision, we would demolish the present building and build a Community Centre, which would include a worship space. As soon as they heard of our plans Birmingham City Council had our building listed, meaning that demolition was no longer possible. We looked at other alternatives, but the cost of refurbishment meant that we felt we could not justify that expense just to remain in the building.

Whilst we contemplated our future, we decided to move worship 'up the road' to Hall Green Methodist Church and we started worshipping together and the decision was made to sell the Sparkhill building. In September of that year, we signed a Declaration of Intent and five years later a Sharing Agreement which committed us to shared use of the Methodist building and the responsibility for it. Finally on 19th October 2014, we adopted a new constitution and officially became Hall Green United Community Church.

It was my privilege to serve on the committees that brought together our three denominations into one church. I am proud to say that in these ten years we have upheld the traditions and practises of those denominations under the stewardship of both Moravian and Methodist ministers. As I write this in 2024, we are actively pursuing the calling of our first URC minister. So here I am, whose faith life began as an Anglican, then became a Congregationalist, later a member of the URC. Then the Moravians came along, and I became a Moravian lay preacher and now I hold membership of the URC, The Moravian Church and the Methodist Church, the latter who honoured me by accepting my Moravian lay preaching training and enrolling me as a Methodist local preacher.

The coming together of the churches has brought many benefits and, certainly for me, no disadvantages. As a Local Ecumenical Partnership, we are a separate registered charity and run by our own elected Trustees. This gives us a degree of independence from our parent churches, enabling us to use the best practises and materials from them and making them our own. Personally, it also meant that we were introduced to a new group of Christians who shared their testimony and wisdom. Chief if these is my friend Keith Dennis, quite simply the wisest man I know. A retired headmaster who has trained many local preachers, he and I have become almost a 'double act'. We have preached together, put on shows together and, most importantly, laughed together for the past 14 years or so. Lynn and I are proud to call Keith and his wife Barbara, friends.

The other advantage of being in our church like ours is the support that is given when needed. Through my two major illnesses, I was surrounded and upheld by my friends at HGUCC, as well as my secular friends. My faith has been extended by knowing too many people to mention all by name, but some have to be name-checked. Rev. Peter Bates (Methodist) and Rev. David Howarth (Moravian) were the two clerics who first brought our congregations together. It was an honour for me to celebrate this with a speech at Moravian Synod with both of them present. Rev. Nick Jones (Methodist) who became our minister later is one of the most supportive people I know and, without doubt, the best preacher I have ever heard.

Among the laity, people like Linda Ramdharry, Julia Parkes, the Dickens duo, Val and Brian, my old school friend Alan Perkins and many others have impressed me with their dedication to service and the welfare of the church and community. Lynn and I have been truly blessed by knowing them.

Apart from my brush with cancer, one of the biggest challenges for us was Covid and lockdown. With my health record, I was immediately placed on the 'at-risk' list and told to isolate immediately. As usual, family back-up was at hand and, until we were able to arrange home deliveries from Tesco, sister-in-law Jill did our shopping. There was a minor embarrassment in that because of my listing, the local authority kept delivering food parcels to our door. A lovely thought, but unnecessary in our case. It took some time to get these stopped and it was an indication of how local government was forced to react that when I finally got through to someone in Birmingham City Council, the young lady apologised and told me that she normally worked in waste management!

I asked Lynn about her favourite parts of retirement, and she said there were three. Firstly, being able to stay in bed on weekday mornings and secondly, discovering the will power to drink wine only at weekends, holidays excluded.

The third benefit is the one we both agree on. The privilege of welcoming three new grandchildren into the family. Jessica was born before we retired but was later joined by her sister Tegan, daughter to Louise and Jon. Cora was the first of Caitlin and Dunstan's daughters, with Laurel becoming our youngest granddaughter. The joy of watching them grow and develop is, simply, one of the best things in my life. The pleasure of their company, the thrill of sharing their accomplishments and the wonderful feeling of hearing, "I love you, granddad" make me as happy as I have ever been. Having and raising my wonderful son and daughter was special, but grandchildren are different. Without the pressure of parenthood, you are able to see them grow without having any responsibly.

Of course, there have been downsides. One of the side-effects of growing old, is that you outlive people you love. Over the years we have lost family and good friends. The original Silver Ten now number just six, for example. I have had the honour of presiding at many funerals over the years giving me the opportunity to celebrate the lives of many loved ones. I cannot tell you how special this is and how grateful I am to my friend, Rev. Graham Spicer for his encouragement when I was first asked to take a funeral. Many years later, Graham himself was dying and phoned me up. "There is only one person that I would trust with my funeral,", he said, "but I'll be dead so you will have to do!".

And that seems a good story to end this memoir. There are more stories I could tell, more people I could mention but I go back to my art tutor's words. "You always feel that there is more you can do with a painting, but the time comes when you have to step away and say, it's done." So this is done. I have had a fortunate life, blessed in so many ways, but mainly by Lynn to whom this is dedicated.

Printed in Great Britain
by Amazon